Islamic
Fundamentalism

Introducing Islam

Islamic Fundamentalism

Kim Whitehead

Produced by OTTN Publishing, Stockton, New Jersey

Mason Crest Publishers
370 Reed Road
Broomall, PA 19008
www.masoncrest.com

Copyright © 2004 by Mason Crest Publishers. All rights reserved.
Printed and bound in the Hashemite Kingdom of Jordan.

First printing

1 3 5 7 9 8 6 4 2

Library of Congress Cataloging-in-Publication Data

Whitehead, Kim.
  Islamic fundamentalism / Kim Whitehead.
      v. cm. — (Introducing Islam)
  Includes bibliographical references and index.
  Contents: Defining Islamic fundamentalism — Islamic fundamentalism in
the modern age — The Iranian revolution — Saudi Arabia — The Arab
world — Asia — Sub-Saharan Africa — The Western response.
   ISBN 1-59084-703-2
  1. Islamic fundamentalism—Juvenile literature. [1. Islamic
fundamentalism. 2. Islamic countries.] I. Title. II. Series.
  BP166.14.F85W47 2004
  297'.09'04—dc22
                          2003013295

Contents

Introduction

The central belief of Islam, one of the world's major religions, is contained in a simple but powerful phrase: "There is no god but Allah, and Muhammad is His prophet." The Islamic faith, which emerged from the Arabian desert in the seventh century C.E., has become one of the world's most important and influential religions.

Within a century after the death of the prophet Muhammad, Islam had spread throughout the Arabian Peninsula into Europe, Africa, and Asia. Today Islam is the world's fastest-growing religion and Muslims can be found throughout the globe. There are about 1.25 billion Muslims, which means that approximately one of every five people follows Islam. The global total of believers has surpassed two older religions, Hinduism and Buddhism; only Christianity has more followers.

Muslims can also be found in North America. Many Muslims have immigrated to the United States and Canada, and large numbers of people—particularly African Americans—have converted to Islam since the 1960s. Today, there are an estimated 6 million Muslims in the United States, with an additional half-million Muslims in Canada.

Despite this growing popularity, many people in the West are uninformed about Islam. For many Americans, their only exposure to this important religion, with its glorious history and rich culture, is through news reports about wars in Muslim countries, terrorist attacks, or fundamentalist denunciations of Western corruption.

The purpose of the INTRODUCING ISLAM series is to provide an objective examination of Islam and give an overview of what Muslims believe, how they practice their faith, and what values they hold most important. Four volumes in particular focus on Islamic beliefs and religious practices. *Islam: The Basics* answers the essential questions about the faith and provides information about the major sects. *Islam, Christianity, and Judaism* describes and explains the similarities and differences between these three great monotheistic religions. *Heroes and Holy Places* gives information about such important figures as Muhammad and Saladin, as well as shrines like Mecca and Jerusalem. *Islamic Fundamentalism* focuses on the emergence of the Islamist movement during the 20th century, the development of an Islamist government in Iran, and the differences between Islamists and moderates in such countries as Algeria, Indonesia, and Egypt.

Two volumes in the series explore Islam in the United States, and the relationship between the Muslim world and the West. *The American Encounter with Islam* provides specific history about Muslims in North America from the 17th century until the present, and traces the development of uniquely American sects like the Nation of Islam. *Muslims and the West* attempts to put the encounter between two important civilizations in broader perspective from a historical point of view.

Recent statistical data is extensively provided in two volumes, in order to discuss life in the Muslim world. *Who Are the Muslims?* is a geopolitical survey that explores the many different cultures that can be found in the Muslim world, as well as the different types of Islamic governments. *What Muslims Think and How They Live* uses information collected in a landmark survey of the Islamic world by the Gallup Organization, as well as other socioeconomic data, to examine Muslim attitudes toward a variety of questions and issues.

As we enter a new century, cultural and political tensions between Muslims and non-Muslims continue. Now more than ever, it is important for people to learn more about their neighbors of all faiths. It is only through education and tolerance that we will be able to build a new world in which fear and mistrust are replaced with brotherhood and peace.

Broadly speaking, Islamic fundamentalists advocate a return to their religion's seventh-century roots, and they want Islam to be the organizing principle for all aspects of life, including politics, law, and social relations. Beyond these and a few other shared goals, however, the character of Islamic fundamentalism tends to vary by region and culture.

Defining Islamic Fundamentalism

Islam is the youngest of the major world religions, but it is also the fastest growing: in many areas of the world, including Europe and the United States, the number of Muslims is increasing rapidly. In this global context, Muslims exhibit as many differences among themselves as do Christians. Different groups of Muslims express and practice their beliefs in different ways.

Muslims do, however, hold some common beliefs and consider themselves a worldwide community (*umma*) unified in devotion to Allah. (*Allah* is the Arabic word for God.) Regardless of where they live, Muslims share a faith in a single God and revere their holy text, the Qur'an. They also take very seriously both their moral responsibility and their accountability before God, and they believe their faith should inform all areas of life.

The belief that religion cannot be separated from any other part of life was an important part of the teachings of the prophet Muhammad in the seventh century, and for hundreds of years this belief buttressed a great Islamic civilization that extended its power through the Middle East and into Asia, Africa, and Europe. But the rise of European power and the era of Western colonialism in the 18th, 19th, and 20th centuries eroded Islamic institutions and the long tradition of cultural and intellectual unity among Muslims, leading to a sense of powerlessness and loss. In this new context, Muslims adapted differing viewpoints on the role of Islam in political and social life.

During the colonial period, Muslims developed a range of responses to Western expansion. Muslim reformers argued that Muslims should not simply accept or reject Western ideals, but should reinterpret traditional Islamic institutions and law in order to adapt to the contemporary situation. These Muslims were known broadly as Islamic modernists. Other thinkers and activists argued that the only path to survival and prosperity in the modern era was to fully Westernize, to adopt secular modes of government and public life. Others began to call for a return to the roots of the Islamic faith as a way to recover a sense of identity and reclaim power for Muslim societies. They said that the only way to revitalize Muslim societies was to reestablish religious legal authority in every sphere of life. These Muslims have been widely referred to as Islamic fundamentalists, and their response to the pressures of modernity gained momentum during the 20th century.

In response to the decline of Islamic political and cultural power, fundamentalists blame Muslims themselves for straying from the straight path of Islam. They also say secular political and moral systems (particularly from the West) are unjust and bankrupt and that they erode Islamic institutions and the Muslim way of life. Islamic fundamentalists want to rid their religion of all such corruption, both among Muslims themselves and from external influ-

Islamic fundamentalism arose in part as a reaction against Western political and cultural dominance. Today ambivalence toward Western—and, in particular, U.S.—influences pervades many Arab societies.

ences. In theory, they see any innovation in Islam beyond the practices set forth by Muhammad and his earliest followers in the seventh century, as well as all non-Muslim practices, as a potential threat to their faith. Fundamentalists propose Islam as a comprehensive system that governs all of life, and many of them support the idea of national government based on the *Sharia* (Islamic law). Since the mid-1900s, and particularly since the 1960s, these fundamentalist views have had enormous effects on Muslims themselves and on political and social realities in countries around the world.

But while fundamentalists decry reformist and modernist Muslims' openness to the West, their own approaches have sometimes themselves been shaped by Western ideals. This is perhaps nowhere more evident than in contemporary attitudes toward the Sharia. Through the centuries, most Muslims have viewed the Sharia not as a code of fixed rules that govern behavior, but rather as the path toward knowledge of God's will and the way to achieve God's justice on earth. The Sharia includes not only rules, but also the methods of interpretation judges use to determine those rules; throughout the Islamic world, judges deal with important issues in local Muslim communities and develop interpretations based on the Qur'an and the example of the prophet Muhammad relevant to the context. The Sharia is not a codified, fixed set of laws enforced by a central government. However, with the advent of the nation-state and colonialism—together with the idea of a standard, fixed law written for an entire country—some Muslims' ideas about the Sharia also changed. Many fundamentalists came to view the Sharia as a fixed set of laws that should uniformly govern an entire nation. The Sharia as a fixed entity then increasingly took on a symbolic role as fundamentalists sought to build support against Western cultural and political control in Muslim countries.

Because Muslims believe the Qur'an records the exact words of God, great emphasis is placed on studying, memorizing, and reciting the holy book in the classical Arabic in which it was originally revealed to the prophet Muhammad. That language can be difficult to master, even for native speakers of modern Arabic. Shown here is a Qur'an student in Djenné, a town in the West African country of Mali.

THE FUNDAMENTALIST WORLDVIEW

While defining Islamic fundamentalism as a whole is a useful exercise, it is helpful to remember that the phenomenon takes as many different shapes within Islam as do culturally specific Islamic expressions of faith. Fundamentalists do not all share the same socioeconomic background, nor do they subscribe to one global set of objectives. Modern fundamentalism is not a movement exclusively, or even predominantly, of the poor, uneducated, and marginalized within the Islamic world. Rather, it flourishes particularly among the educated middle classes and in certain respects is a product of the spread of literacy. Nor do all fundamentalists strive for the same political goals. Many join moderate political parties to seek changes through the government; a relative few, such as the extremist Osama bin Laden, vow to wage war at all costs against both non-Muslims and any Muslims thought to support Western ideals and governments.

It is also important to understand the complex historical context in which contemporary Islamic fundamentalism developed. After the end of European colonialism in the Islamic world, the growth of fundamentalism was hastened by numerous events: the founding of the State of Israel in 1948, U.S. intervention in the Middle East, the end of the Cold War, the failure of nationalist governments in the Arab world, and the process of globalization, in which clear distinctions between the East and the West have disappeared.

In contrast to fundamentalists, modernists seek an environment in which modern ideas can coexist with Muslim ideals and faith. Many moderate modernists appeal directly to the Qur'an, the *Hadith* (the body of traditions and sayings ascribed to Muhammad), and Islamic history to advocate democracy, human rights, and a largely secular society. Secularists, in contrast, seek to distance government from Islamic institutions and to embrace completely nonreligious models of national identity and economic development.

But fundamentalism and modernism are both responses to

pressures on Islam in the modern world—pressures from without to accept secular views of the relationship between society, government, and religion, and pressures from within to refuse to change centuries-old traditions in the face of contemporary realities. Modernists seek to accommodate new ideas within Islam, while fundamentalists seek to return to the core vision of Islam they believe to be set forth in the Qur'an and Hadith.

Numerous scholars of Islam have attempted to identify the basic characteristics of fundamentalist Islamic thought. It is hard to settle on a comprehensive list, but the following beliefs are common:

Islam is a comprehensive system that directs all aspects of life, including politics and society.

To restore purity to Islam, Muslims must rely solely on the Qur'an and the examples set forth in the first days of Islam by Muhammad and his companions. Therefore, Islam has no room for academic speculation about faith or law.

Muslims must reject both secular states in Muslim countries and the Western models they follow, which are unjust and spiritually corrupt.

The rule of Islamic law is God's will, and therefore Muslims must replace Western-based legal systems with the Sharia and the rulings of Islamic religious authorities.

Muslims can use the tools of modernity (science and technology), but only in subservience to Islamic values and codes of behavior.

DEFINING THE KEY TERMS

The term *fundamentalism* actually refers to any effort to purify a religion by laying out the fundamentals of that religion and expecting individuals and even whole societies to abide by them. Fundamentalists have emerged in every major religion in the modern era. The term *fundamentalism* was in fact coined to describe the call for a return to the roots of Christianity made by some Protestant Christians in the United States during the 1920s. It came into wide use for Islamic groups only after the Iranian revolution in 1979.

Though *fundamentalism* is still the most widely used term for the modern efforts to purify Islam, other terms are used frequently as well. These include *revivalism, Islamism, resurgence, traditionalism*, and *renewal*. Increasingly, *Islamism* is used in journalistic and scholarly accounts of the phenomenon. *Fundamentalism* is often used interchangeably with *militant extremism*, but the latter term refers specifically to the beliefs of fundamentalist groups who advocate violence as a means to bring about their proposed reforms. These militant groups are a minority among Islamic fundamentalists. Most fundamentalists work through religious institutions and political parties to enact changes peacefully.

Another term widely associated with Islamic fundamentalism is the Arabic word *jihad*, which is often interpreted to mean "holy war" but literally translates as "struggle" and has a long and complex history of use within Islam. In fact, the legal scholars (*ulama*) who formulated most of Islamic law by the 11th century did not specify the concept of jihad as holy war. The Qur'an simply calls Muslims to "struggle in the path of God." Traditionally, the ulama distinguished between the Greater Jihad, which is the effort of the individual to become a better Muslim, and the Lesser Jihad, which referred to the struggle against enemies to defend the oppressed and establish justice. The majority of the *ulama* argued that Muslims should fight others only when they threaten Muslims. The *ulama* did, however, condemn any who acted with indiscriminate violence. The *ulama* called these rebels *muharibs* ("those who fight society") and defined them as terrorists who secretly carry out violent acts against innocent people and thus keep the entire society in fear.

However, as colonialism eroded traditional institutions and beliefs and as secular, nationalist governments further undermined the role of Islamic authority, the conditions emerged for a new, more militant definition of *jihad*. Increasing incursions by Western powers led to a loss of self-esteem among Muslims at large. The resulting despair spurred many young Muslims to seek justice. Thus, the new definition of *jihad* as "holy war" pointedly illustrates the political nature of contemporary Islamic fundamentalism as it has taken shape in the past 40 years.

Islamic Fundamentalism in the Modern Age

From the time of Muhammad, Muslims believed that the faithfulness of the *umma* resulted in the expansion of Islamic civilization. But after the enormous territorial and cultural gains of the Abbasid period (750–1258), the empire broke into a scattered collection of kingdoms. Battles with the Europeans during the Crusades in the 11th and 12th centuries and with the Mongols in the 13th century left Islamic forces in further disarray.

Around 1300, however, a new Islamic power began to rise: the Ottoman Empire. From their home base in Anatolia in what is now Turkey, the Ottomans spread their influence outward in a series of conquests. By the mid-1500s the Ottoman Empire stretched from the Middle East and North Africa through Mesopotamia and southeastern Europe. Although a significant number

17

of Muslims remained outside Ottoman rule—especially in India, Iran (Persia), and parts of Africa and Southeast Asia—the empire was the center of Islamic civilization and power for hundreds of years. Within it were the holy cities of Mecca, Medina, and Jerusalem and the leading cultural centers of Istanbul, Baghdad, Cairo, and Damascus.

By 1600, European nations had begun to seriously challenge the power of the Ottoman Empire. Over the next three centuries, the Europeans would wear down and ultimately eclipse the Ottomans militarily and commercially.

Changes in the global economy, as well as European innova-

Although the Ottoman Empire dominated much of the Islamic world politically and culturally for centuries, significant Muslim populations remained outside its domain. For example, the Mughal Empire flourished in India from the early 16th to the mid-18th century. Shown here is a view of the famous Taj Mahal, constructed by the Mughal ruler Shah Jahan as a mausoleum for his wife. It was completed in 1653.

tions, helped tip the balance in favor of Europe. With advances in navigation and shipping, the traditional silk routes through the Middle East and Central Asia, which the Ottomans controlled, were no longer vital. Exploration and colonization of the Americas resulted in an influx of cheap resources, and industrialization shifted commercial power to Europe. The *sultans* of the Ottoman Empire found themselves increasingly in debt to European powers, and on the battlefield their military forces had little success against the more sophisticated weaponry developed by the Europeans.

By the late 1700s, Western ideas began to seep into the empire as Europeans continued to expand their military and commercial power at the expense of the Ottomans. Many among the *ulama* concluded that Muslims had strayed from the straight path of Islam. To turn back the Europeans, they believed, Muslims would have to return to their faith.

From their origins in the seventh century, the *ulama* had developed into a special Muslim class, with the authority to study the Qur'an and the Hadith and discern God's will for the Islamic community. The *ulama* are not priests, but laymen trained in religious doctrine and prepared to transmit it. As Islam developed and spread, the *ulama* relied on the Sharia as they made legal rulings governing all aspects of Muslim life, which they applied as judges. The *ulama* became the leaders of Islam's mosques and seminaries and had extensive control in a vast religion that functioned with little central organization. As Western thought and customs continued to filter into the Ottoman Empire through the 1800s, however, the *ulama* found themselves increasingly isolated and their powers reduced until they were confined to issuing legal opinions on personal life only.

Meanwhile, as European powers occupied Muslim territories— the French in North Africa, the Russians in Central Asia, the British in Egypt and India, the Dutch in Southeast Asia—the Ottoman Empire implemented military and bureaucratic reforms and went through a series of failed experiments with Western-style representative government. By 1900 much of the Muslim world was under some form of European control, and World War I finally swept away the remnants of the Ottoman Empire two decades later. With Britain and France splitting the remaining Ottoman lands after the war, the last Islamic empire had been destroyed. The global Muslim community was devastated by the loss.

During the Ottoman Empire's long decline, Islamic thinkers and activists had tried to envision a path back to Islam's former glory. By the late 19th century, both modernist and fundamentalist responses to the crisis in Islam were emerging. They shared the ultimate goal of beating back Western expansion but differed greatly in approach. The modernists sought to forge a relationship between Islam and Western models of government and development. Islamic legal reformers joined this trend, which in the end actually eroded the influence of the Sharia, Islamic judges, and the *ulama*. The fundamentalists, by contrast, organized in opposition to it.

THE REFORMERS

The roots of Islamic modernism are epitomized in the work of certain key thinkers, all of whom insisted that Muslims needed to reform their traditions in order to regain their lost power. These thinkers believed Islam could use Western patterns of government because similar patterns had in fact once been central to Islamic rule, but had been lost through the years.

Jamal al-Din Afghani (1838–1897), a Persian, traveled widely among Islamic lands and often supported groups resistant to European expansion and control. He said that scientific inquiry had been a key part of Islamic civilization and that eliminating it was in part to blame for the decline in Islam's status. Rather than reject Western scientific advances, Afghani wanted Muslims and the *ulama* in particular to locate the secrets of Western strength and use them to their advantage. He also advocated for parliamentary forms of government, which he identified with the traditional Islamic practice of consultation (*shura*), as well as a new emphasis on science and technology.

Afghani maintained that Muslims must remain rooted in the practices set forth by Muhammad and the first believers (*salafiyya*). He did not suggest, however, a simple return to the traditional interpretations of Islam, but rather advocated new interpretations that would enable Muslims to respond to their changing world. He sought to reintroduce the concept of *ijtihad*, individual interpretation of the law, and to replace the practice of *taqlid*, the simple imitation of the law as set forth by the *ulama* in the first several centuries after Muhammad. The practice of *ijtihad* would enable Muslims to preserve their core traditions while reinterpreting sections of the law to reflect modern realities.

With support from the Ottoman sultan, Afghani proposed a Pan-Islamic coalition of countries and regions that reflected the idea of the *umma*. He saw this as important because in their colonies the Europeans were establishing the boundaries of future nation-states, a foreign concept in lands once united under the rule of Islamic empires. He believed Muslims must reassert their unity in order to adapt to the pressures of the modern era.

Afghani's Egyptian student Muhammad Abduh (1849–1905) was a leading member of the *ulama* who said that faith and reason go hand in hand and that the decline of Islam could be blamed on the unwillingness of the *ulama* to consider new interpretations of tradition. Abduh maintained that certain laws (especially those regarding worship) should go unchanged but that laws about family and society should be reinterpreted with changing historical conditions. He proposed more education for women, for example, and argued against polygamy.

Like Afghani and his followers, India's Sayyid Ahmad Khan (1817–1898) proposed a reinterpretation of Islamic traditions, but he went one step further: rather than suggesting that Islam could coexist with reason and science, he believed Islam, reason, and science were inextricably bound together and thus the Qur'an and Hadith should be interpreted in light of modern scientific thinking. His political analysis, however, did not stretch beyond British rule in India. He thought any attempts at Pan-Islamic unity were not feasible, and he suggested that Indian Muslims needed to accept and adapt to the reality of British power in their country, something for which Afghani criticized him.

These modernist reformers all proposed a reinterpretation of Islam rather than an uncritical acceptance of tradition, and they sought a synthesis of Islamic tenets and the scientific and intellectual developments of modernity. From North Africa east to Indonesia, modernists acted on their ideas with mixed results. Melding tradition with modern ideas was not easy in practice, especially since the conservative *ulama* still governed the academic and legal institutions of Islam, which gave the reformers no platform for enacting their ideas. It was also difficult to develop leadership roles among the secularists, who ended up heading the new Muslim countries. In most nation-states gaining their independence from colonial powers, secular legislatures set up the legal codes.

THE ROOTS OF THE FUNDAMENTALIST RESPONSE

The argument that Muslims must not stray from the straight path of Islam is almost as old as Islam itself. Only 25 years after the prophet Muhammad's death, the Kharijis became the first dissenters in Islam, asserting a literal interpretation of the Qur'an and an ultra-strict delineation between Muslims, who prove their faith in their behavior, and non-Muslims. In the Kharijis' view, Muslims who were seen to have compromised their faith had to be excluded from the Islamic community and could even be punished by death.

As Islamic institutions and law developed over the following centuries, many religious reformers (*mujaddids*) appealed to this vision of "pure" Islam. Dismayed by the Mongols' defeat of the Abbasid **Caliphate**, the legal scholar Taqi al-Din Ahmad ibn

Taymiyya (1268–1328) called for a strict, literal interpretation of the Qur'an and Hadith as the only way to restore Islamic purity and Islamic power. He issued a legal opinion (*fatwa*) condemning the Mongols because they professed Islam but did not follow the Sharia and calling on faithful Muslims not to obey their Mongol rulers.

Ibn Taymiyya's fatwa greatly affected the thinking of Muhammad ibn Abd al-Wahhab (1703–1792). Al-Wahhab was highly critical of what he saw as corruption in Islamic society on the Arabian Peninsula, which he said had returned to a pre-Islamic state of ignorance. He called for a literal interpretation of the Qur'an, considered most of the Sharia a corruption of authentic Islam, and did not recognize the legitimacy of the long-established schools of Islamic law. Al-Wahhab called for *ijtihad*, and indeed his emphasis on this concept foreshadowed the work of Muslim reformers like Afghani and Abduh. Al-Wahhab's goal, however, was not to reform Islam to reflect new ideas and practices, but rather to return the Islamic way of life to the "golden age" of Islam, when Muhammad and his companions in Medina set forth infallible codes of belief and conduct. Al-Wahhab and the Arabian tribal chief Muhammad ibn Saud declared war on all people they considered unfaithful to true Islam. Though defeated by the Ottoman Empire, they laid the foundation for the modern state of Saudi Arabia and set an example that would inspire later fundamentalist groups.

Throughout the 19th century, numerous rebellions against colonial powers used Islamic language and symbols to legitimize their cause, while other movements actively called for a return to pure Islam as part of their struggle. In West Africa, for instance, fundamentalist movements organized with the goal of returning Islam to political power and enforcing strict adherence to the Sharia. In countries like Nigeria, Somalia, and Sudan, fundamentalists staged reform efforts and outright rebellions, most of which were brutally suppressed. Similar rebellions occurred in India and western China.

INTO THE 20TH CENTURY

The Western colonial presence continued in much of the Muslim world into the early 1900s. Twentieth-century fundamentalism first developed in response to Western colonialism and strengthened as Muslim modernists developed patterns of self-rule using nationalist, secular models.

The Muslim Brotherhood took the lead in the Arab world. It was established in Egypt in 1928 by Hasan al-Banna (1906–1949), who used Islamic symbols to build greater unity among Egyptians in resistance to the British colonial presence and later developed extensive social programs for Egyptians living under independent but secular rule. The Islamic Society of India, founded in 1941 by Mawlana Mawdudi (1903–1979), shared much the same approach.

After independence, many of the new countries used Western parliamentary forms of government; some aligned themselves with democratic capitalism (such as Turkey and Tunisia), while others developed forms of socialism (such as Egypt, Syria, Iraq, and Libya). The new nationalist governments understood the influence of Islam in society—many leaders appealed to citizens by using Islamic language and symbols—but they kept the walls between politics and religion intact. In only a few countries did Islamic religious authorities legitimize monarchies (Morocco, Jordan, Oman, and the Malayan States) or retain real power (Yemen, Saudi Arabia).

In the aftermath of colonial domination, however, the new secular governments struggled, beset by corruption, mismanagement, and continued Western influence. High unemployment and poverty rates increased the feelings of loss and low self-esteem among Muslim citizens, while the rapid pace of modernization jeopardized traditional Islamic values and practices.

Both al-Banna and Mawdudi opposed the *ulama* for collaborating with secular governments, and the modernist reformers for relying too much on Western ideals. Both argued that every realm of life should be directed by Islamic principles. Al-Banna established the

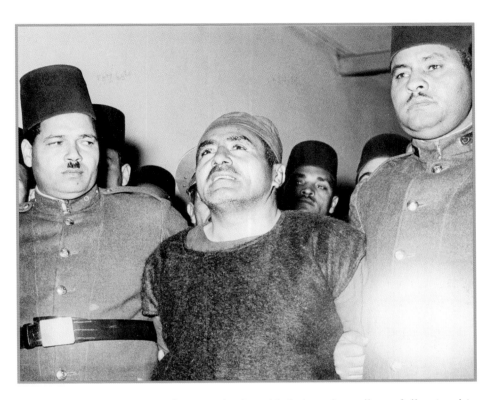

A member of Egypt's Muslim Brotherhood is led to the gallows following his conviction for a 1954 plot to assassinate President Gamal Abdel Nasser. Nasser banned the fundamentalist organization and ordered a ruthless crackdown on its members, but the Brotherhood remained a significant force in Egyptian society.

Muslim Brotherhood when he was only 22, arguing that the *ulama* had failed to resist the spiritual decay and foreign values brought by Westernization. Furthermore, he maintained, while Britain had granted Egypt's independence in 1922, it still controlled the country.

Al-Banna assailed the new Egyptian government's corruption, and, though he was not against democracy itself, he thought the Western patterns of government the Egyptian leaders had imported were imposing values that common Egyptians did not share. Islam and the Qur'an offered everything Muslims needed, said al-Banna, so they did not need to turn to the West for ideas about how to govern their society. He also condemned the materialism he saw in both capitalist and communist societies, asserting that it threatened

Muslims' spiritual well-being even as it created deep divisions between the ruling elite and average citizens. He emphasized non-violent jihad as the only way to bring revival to Muslims and return Islam to its rightful place in the world. In its appeal to Egyptian Muslims as a whole, the Muslim Brotherhood under al-Banna founded broad social welfare programs to provide an Islamic alternative to the Egyptian government.

Mawdudi was driven in large part by his concern that Indian Muslims be granted independence to govern their own affairs and not be subsumed in a new Hindu-dominated, secular Indian government. He maintained that Islam and nationalism were incompatible, and that their faith alone bound Muslims together as a community. In the beginning, he did not support the creation of Pakistan as a solution to the Indian Muslim problem, for he rightly realized that it, too, would be a secular experiment. Unlike al-Banna, Mawdudi always envisioned change from the top down, arguing until his death for an Islamic state in Pakistan. Perhaps Mawdudi's central contribution to later fundamentalist movements was his interpretation of the concept of jihad as the struggle for a Muslim revolution in the entire world order.

The governments of Egypt and Pakistan saw the Muslim Brotherhood and the Islamic Society, respectively, as a radical threat to their secular rule. The Egyptian secret police killed al-Banna in 1949. Egyptian president Gamal Abdel Nasser outlawed the Muslim Brotherhood in 1954. Nasser ordered the imprisonment and torture of numerous Brotherhood leaders and members. Later, after a period of revival under Anwar Sadat, the group was partially banned again. In Pakistan, Mawdudi was kept under surveillance and spent time in prison on several occasions.

Both al-Banna and Mawdudi influenced Sayyid Qutb (1906–1966), a prominent member of the Egyptian Muslim Brotherhood. In his books *In the Shade of the Qur'an*, a multivolume commentary on the Qur'an, and *Milestones*, Qutb provided an in-depth response to the tensions between Islam and the West. Qutb extended Mawdudi's assessment that Western societies were ignorant (*jahili*) of God's will because of their lack of Islamic rule, and as the Egyptian government brutally suppressed the Muslim Brotherhood, he eventually concluded that leaders of Muslim countries also encouraged *jahiliyyah* and must be forcibly removed from power. Qutb based his thinking in part on time he spent in the United States, where he was appalled by what he saw as unbridled materialism, sexual promiscuity, and racism. Qutb also felt that U.S. support for the new state of Israel came at the expense of Muslim interests.

Qutb did not hesitate to identify those committed to Islamic rule as good and those opposed as evil, and the Egyptian government was so concerned about the spread of his radical vision that it declared any citizen caught with a copy of *Milestones* liable for treason. After 10 years in prison, Qutb was executed in 1966 under order from Nasser. His intelligent writings and his refusal to give in to Nasser (he could have avoided death by recanting his writings) remain a strong influence on radical fundamentalists today. His influence is also felt among Muslims in general; *In the Shade of the Qur'an* is still widely read throughout the Islamic world by Muslims of diverse backgrounds and beliefs.

FUNDAMENTALISM AFTER 1960

By the 1960s, frustration with the failures of secular rule in the Muslim world—government corruption, false promises of democracy, ongoing unemployment and poverty—as well as Israel's growing power had eroded Muslim confidence so much that the fundamentalist appeal took on new momentum.

In June 1967, Israel defeated the combined forces of Egypt, Jordan, and Syria in the Six-Day War, creating new longings among Arabs for the glories of past Islamic civilizations. Egypt's modest successes in the 1973 October War with Israel, together with Arab states' imposition of an oil embargo that same year, kindled hope for a new era of Islamic power. But more than any other event, the Iranian revolution of 1979 inspired those Muslims who sought

Islamic renewal. When young militants forced the pro-West shah of Iran into exile and swept the *Ayatollah* Ruhollah Khomeini into power, giving rise to a new Islamic state, great numbers of Muslims rededicated themselves to daily prayer and the Muslim holy days.

Muslims longing for Islamic renewal also developed Islamic media outlets and established reformist Islamic groups, including political parties. Community-based organizations like the Muslim Brotherhood and university student groups increased in size and influence, widening their grassroots work and calling for a gradual conversion to Islamic values and government. Many conservative *ulama*—for instance, those of Cairo's al-Azhar Mosque University —began to advocate the return to pure forms of Islam. At least on a superficial level, secular governments also responded; leaders in numerous Muslim countries increasingly appealed to Islam to enhance their legitimacy and popular support.

Non-militant fundamentalist Islamic organizations increased their participation in the political process in the 1980s and 1990s.

In 1979 massive street protests in Tehran and other Iranian cities helped topple the secular, pro-U.S. regime of Mohammad Reza Pahlavi and bring to power a government dominated by conservative Shiite clerics.

They participated in elections, and in some cases their candidates were elected to high national office. They focused on international issues as well, their top concern being Israel's occupation of Palestinian territories. They also protested the Soviet Union's occupation of Afghanistan, United Nations sanctions against Iraq after the Gulf War, and government repression of Muslims in Bosnia, Chechnya, and Kashmir.

In the meantime, however, militant groups also flourished, attracting new recruits across the Muslim world and especially in Egypt, Lebanon, and Palestine. In Egypt numerous secret groups plotted to overthrow their own government. Muhammad al-Faraj, a member of the group Islamic Jihad, relied heavily on Ibn Taymiyya and Qutb in his manifesto *The Neglected Duty*, in which he interpreted jihad as a violent struggle against corrupt society. He spoke of jihad as the forgotten sixth pillar of Islam and called for armed revolution to overthrow Egypt's secular leaders and install an Islamic state.

Iran backed some militant groups, including Hizbollah, which fought the Israeli occupation of Lebanese territories in the 1980s. The groups Hamas and Islamic Jihad formed in the Israeli-occupied West Bank and Gaza Strip to fight for a Palestinian state and began dispatching suicide bombers to attack Israeli targets. And in Afghanistan, the Wahhabist mindset of Osama bin Laden and other U.S.-backed rebels ignited a new militancy in the Arabs who had gathered there to fight Soviet occupation. Bin Laden later became the leader of al-Qaeda, which carried out the September 11, 2001, suicide attacks on the United States. These groups made up only a small minority of Muslim fundamentalists, but the threat they posed to their own and Western countries in the eyes of many overshadowed the quiet work done by less radical fundamentalist groups.

A closer examination of the full range of the work of fundamentalist groups, both moderate and militant, in different Muslim countries and regions will provide a more complete understanding of just how modern fundamentalism has affected Muslims and how Western governments have responded to it.

Large crowds turned out for this rally in Tehran marking the 22nd anniversary of Iran's Islamic Revolution. But by the early years of the 21st century, dissatisfaction with the government's restrictive social policies and economic mismanagement was believed to be widespread, particularly among the young.

The Iranian Revolution

As followers of Shia Islam, Iranians had long seen themselves as a separate people with a tradition of fighting injustice, and they set themselves further apart by taking on the West and developing a popular movement for an Islamic state. The Iranian revolution of 1979 in turn did more than any other event in modern-day Islam to spread fundamentalism through the global Islamic community and alert the rest of the world to its influence.

HISTORY OF IRAN

With the advent of the Safavid dynasty in 1501, Iran (long called Persia) became a unified independent state.

The first leader of the dynasty declared himself *shah* (king), a title dating from the pre-Islamic era, and proclaimed Twelver Shiism the official religion. Patriotism came easily to the Iranians because they were sharply aware of their pre-Islamic history and maintained their own language (Persian). For the next 150 years, Iran fought the Sunni-dominated Ottoman Empire for control over the Middle East.

The shahs developed very extravagant lifestyles, however, and decline set in. Throughout the 1800s, Russia and Britain fought for control over the Iranian government and outlying Iranian territories, because the country lay between the boundaries of their empires. By 1900 many Iranians supported the idea of national laws in the form of a constitution to curb the shahs' excesses and protect the country from foreign influence. In 1905 demonstrations and strikes forced the shah to submit to a freely elected parliament (the Majlis). Fearing this new independence, Britain financed the exploration for oil in southwest Iran in 1908 and bought a majority share in the country's petroleum industry, while Russia backed royalist attempts to dissolve the elected government.

After World War I, as Britain continued efforts to control the country, a prominent nationalist organized a successful *coup* and declared himself the new shah, renaming himself Reza Shah Pahlavi. The new shah initiated an ambitious modernization scheme, developing industry, infrastructure, and public education, and he sent many Iranians to Europe for training. A professional middle class and a new working class emerged, but the shah's repression of his political enemies increasingly alienated the general population.

During World War II, after Britain and the Soviet Union became allies, they invaded Iran, sent the shah into exile, and with help from the United States took control of Iran's communication and railroad systems. The shah's son, Mohammad Reza Pahlavi, succeeded him and allowed the parliamentary government to continue, though it had little effective power. In the 1940s reformer Mohammad Mosaddeq campaigned against Western control over

Mohammad Mosaddeq, a champion of nationalizing Iran's oil industry and a frequent critic of the shah, served as prime minister between 1951 and 1953, when he was ousted by pro-shah forces supported by the U.S. Central Intelligence Agency.

Iran's economy and against the shah's dictatorship. He led a highly popular movement to turn the oil industry over to the national government, and in 1951 the Majlis nationalized the oil industry and appointed Mosaddeq prime minister. Britain retaliated with a blockade on Iranian oil exports, which took a devastating toll on the economy. As the Cold War geared up, the United States—perceiving Iran as a key front for preventing Soviet expansion—sent Central Intelligence Agency (CIA) operatives to help overthrow Mosaddeq and restore the shah's power. The United States believed that a weak democracy in Iran might invite Soviet intervention in that country's affairs. Under a new agreement, British, Dutch, French, and U.S. companies each gained a share of Iranian oil profits.

With the support of his Western allies, the shah established the secret police known as SAVAK to control opposition, and in 1961 he dissolved the Majlis. He continued modernization efforts, but his land reform program did little to help the rural poor, and while his industrial and public works projects did expand the middle class, the migration of poor villagers to the cities in search of jobs

Mohammad Reza Pahlavi with his second wife, Queen Soraya, 1962. The shah did much to modernize his country and improve its educational system, but his ruthless repression of political opponents and his extravagant lifestyle alienated many of his subjects and helped sow the seeds of his downfall.

led to large slums and degraded living conditions. The shah did not pursue any parallel political reforms; Iran had developed a superior school system, for example, but its well-educated graduates had no real freedom of speech. The shah also gladly accepted military aid from the United States to keep a check on Soviet expansion in the region. When Iran became one of the world's largest exporters of oil, second only to Saudi Arabia, oil revenues provided ample funding for the shah's programs, but the newfound wealth did not trickle down to the middle and working classes.

THE MAKING OF A REVOLUTION

Many of the country's intellectuals and professionals attended college in the West and grew concerned about being too dependent on the United States. Meanwhile, religious leaders, the middle-class shop owners of the *bazaars* (*bazaari*), and the working class saw the modernization and the shah's repressive policies as a threat to their religious heritage and national sovereignty. These groups all called for Islamic reforms as key to real change in Iran. However, they did not share the same emphasis on the role of the *ulama* or the same attitudes toward modern practices. The religious and secular groups ultimately had different goals: the religious leaders wanted an emphasis on Islam and an Islamic state, while the others simply wanted to preserve the identity and cultural heritage of Iran and the Shiites.

The country's university students also grew increasingly critical of the shah's *autocratic* rule. Various student groups were repressed by the SAVAK, and many eventually espoused *Marxism* and called for a communist state like that in China or the Soviet Union. The educated middle class was, however, reluctant to participate in a violent struggle. When the Mujahedin-e-Khalq (the People's Combatants) finally attempted an uprising, it did not attract many converts and was brutally put down by the shah's forces.

Ali Shariati (1933–1977), a French-educated writer and lecturer, was a key influence on students and the Mujahedin-e-Khalq. He combined Shiite beliefs and Western science to reinterpret Islam as the religion of the downtrodden—those oppressed by the racist and classist practices of imperialist nations and multinational corporations. He said that waiting on the return of the *Mahdi* (the "Hidden *Imam*" of Shia tradition, who will reappear before Judgment Day) had made Shiites passive, when they should be actively working to usher in the age of the messiah. This interpretation alarmed both the shah and the *ulama*. Shariati also said that the revolution would start with Iranian intellectuals outside the *ulama*, which resonated with Iran's growing professional class and university groups.

But it was, in fact, the *ulama* who held the key to a successful revolution. They were able to organize and mobilize a broader base of support through their extensive network of mosques and mosque leaders (*mullahs*). Life in the bazaars was built around the mosques and the tombs of Shia saints, which are highly venerated and often visited by Shiites. The mullahs were organized in a tight hierarchy under the elite spiritual authorities known as the ayatollahs. They were also financially independent of the government, unlike the *ulama* in countries dominated by Sunni Muslims. The mullahs collected and redistributed the yearly Muslim tax to benefit the poor (*zakat*), administered the additional Shiite tax on income (*khums*), and ran local schools (*madrasas*). In his hostility toward the mullahs, the shah began to require attendance at modern, state-run schools, a move that infuriated the mullahs and increased the religious devotion of average Iranians. In 1971 the shah founded a state-sanctioned group of religious authorities that he hoped would eventually replace the mullahs.

The mullahs were key to the revolution precisely because Islam was the heart of Iranians' non-Western identity; it provided a common heritage and set of values for all the groups working to overthrow the shah. In addition, the Shiite tradition of opposition was a natural fit for the contemporary situation. Over the centuries, Shiites had come to trace their distinct differences from the Sunnis to the problem of who should have succeeded Muhammad as the leader of the *umma* (the Shiites believed it should have been Muhammad's cousin and son-in-law Ali), and Sunni religious authorities had repeatedly rejected Shiite leaders and put down Shiite rebellions. Shiites also developed a belief in the imminent return of the Mahdi, who would usher in an era of complete social harmony and justice. Thus, the Islamic cry to battle injustice and protect the powerless always rang especially true for the Shiites, and Iranian opposition leaders took it as their own. Mosques in cities and towns across the country became sites for meeting and organizing.

But many of the mullahs were uncertain about the revolutionary ideas espoused by one of their colleagues, the Ayatollah Ruhollah Khomeini (1900/1902–1989). Khomeini had become a hero for the Iranian masses after 1962, when he spoke out publicly against the shah's efforts to modernize Iran. He was taken into custody, which caused mass demonstrations in several cities, and was kept under house arrest until 1964. That year, he again criticized the shah, this time for purchasing American weapons and for granting diplomatic immunity to American military personnel in Iran. The shah forced Khomeini into exile, first in Turkey, then in the Shiite holy city of An Najaf in Iraq, and finally in Paris, the city from which he guided the last stages of the revolution.

From outside Iran, Khomeini could speak without fear of reprisal. He condemned the United States for consciously Westernizing Muslim nations and extending its influence by supporting Israel. He also called for Islam to be implemented on a national level in Iran. He rejected Shariati's claim that the mullahs had been ineffective as advisers to the rulers of Iran, and he went a step further, saying that the country should be ruled by Islamic law and that the most qualified national leaders would be the *ulama* themselves.

Khomeini maintained that the highest power should be given to a cleric well versed in Islamic law (a *faqih*). Many of the mullahs inside Iran understood Khomeini to mean himself, and their leader, the grand ayatollah, publicly opposed the idea. Most of the mullahs also opposed the idea of having too much political power; they preferred to continue operating independently of the government, which they believed by nature to be impure.

The exiled Khomeini became a worldwide symbol of opposition to the shah's oppression, though he was also able to communicate with and guide his followers inside Iran. Cassettes of his speeches and copies of his writings were routinely smuggled into Iran through mosques. But, in spite of his popularity, Khomeini did not emerge as the leader of a broad-based opposition movement in Iran until early 1976.

In 1975 a drop in oil prices led to an economic and social crisis in Iran. The shah responded by halting many business practices of the *bazaari* and throwing some of them in prison, a move that only hardened their opposition. He initiated a similar crackdown on the rest of the middle class.

In 1977 the new U.S. president, Jimmy Carter, demanded that the shah respect human rights by opening up government processes and reining in the SAVAK. The shah began to loosen his stranglehold on the country, but this only increased the opposition's demands. The secular middle class rallied the urban working class, adopting the slogan "Death to the Shah," but this coalition did not have the community base it needed to organize widely. The student groups were also weak, their organization damaged by years of repression.

Khomeini soon became the key figure who would hold the opposition together and increase the levels of protest. In early 1978 a Tehran newspaper published a scathing attack on Khomeini,

From exile the Shiite cleric Ayatollah Ruhollah Khomeini, seen here in a 1978 photo, served as the spiritual leader of Iran's Islamic Revolution.

which united all factions of the resistance in his defense. Even those who did not believe in the concept of a *faqih* were so angered by the attack on Khomeini that they rallied to his side.

Through the mullahs, the entire Iranian network of mosques was at Khomeini's disposal. Without their own ways of reaching the masses, the student groups and middle class united behind Khomeini, too. And Khomeini's charisma did provide coherence: he conveyed a direct message of return to Islam, his simple lifestyle stood in stark contrast to the excesses of the shahs, and his long years of organizing from abroad gave him an army of followers within Iran.

Khomeini's brilliance lay in using Islamic rituals to pull opposition forces together. Every public religious gathering became an occasion for protest: his taped speeches were played during Friday prayers at the mosques, ritual processions became demonstrations in the streets, and the devotional activities of Ramadan were harnessed to further energize the movement. Demonstrators routinely united in shouting *"Allahu Akhbar"* ("God is great"). In addition, rather than launch violent attacks on the shah's military forces, Khomeini prohibited Iranian Shiites from attacking their brothers in the military and invited military personnel to join the cause of the revolution. He also avoided any discussion of the concept of the *faqih*, since he knew this would alienate some sectors of the movement, and he used some of Shariati's terminology to draw in socialist students.

From his exile, Khomeini directed his followers in Iran to incite a series of nationwide strikes and demonstrations. These eventually placed so much pressure on the government that the shah was forced to leave the country in January 1979. Khomeini had developed a network of revolutionary committees based in mosques, and they stepped in to act as police and civil authorities. Within weeks, Khomeini had formed a provisional government, and in a national referendum in March, more than 98 percent of Iranians said yes to an Islamic state.

The controversy over how exactly Iran would be ruled began almost immediately. While most welcomed Khomeini's emphasis on open elections and representative government, secular leaders and some religious leaders opposed the idea of the *faqih*, and minorities like the Kurds and Turkomen argued for greater power for the non-Persian parts of the country. By the end of the year, however, Iran had adopted a constitution that declared Khomeini *faqih* for life and specified a president, a prime minister, a representative Majlis, and a 12-member Council of Guardians, which must approve all laws considered by the Majlis. In contrast to Saudi Arabia, Iran had developed an Islamic state with open processes, including separate legislative, executive, and judicial branches; popular election of the president; and an assembly of experts to be convened to select all subsequent *faqihs*.

AFTER THE REVOLUTION

Under Khomeini's leadership, the Islamic Revolutionary Party quickly consolidated its power over the new government, eliminating secular leaders from positions of power. Khomeini himself declared who and what was Islamic, and he eliminated those he deemed un-Islamic from government, military, and educational institutions. He also ruled that Iranian society had to be freed from corrupt practices and thus banned alcohol, gambling, pornography, mixed bathing, and nightclubs. Friday worship became the center of community life, and all Friday prayer leaders were appointed and supervised by Khomeini. The Council of Guardians, made up of six clergy members and six Islamic lawyers, ensured that all legislation passed by the Majlis conformed to Islamic law.

Several significant events hastened the consolidation of Khomeini's power. Militant students seized the U.S. embassy in Tehran in November 1979, ushering in a phase of extreme anti-American sentiment among young Iranians and leading the United States to cut off diplomatic ties with Iran. Iraq invaded Iran in September 1980, as Saddam Hussein called on oil-rich Iranians to resist the new government, but the ensuing war incited patriotism among Iranians that actually benefited Khomeini's regime.

Meanwhile, some Sunni leaders in neighboring countries worried about the ways the Iranian revolution might inspire Muslims in their states. They denounced Shiites as a heretical sect, asserting that Shiites were not true Muslims, and thus attempted to limit the international influence of Iranian revolutionary ideals.

Under Khomeini's leadership, the new Iranian government confiscated the property and wealth of the upper class (now in exile or executed) and nationalized banks and businesses to gain tighter control over the economy. But the Council of Guardians, in alliance with the *bazaaris*, repeatedly defeated further restrictions on property rights, and the government found itself putting down rebellions by socialist groups, the only remaining voice of the urban poor.

The Iranian government also faced numerous internal struggles

An anti-U.S. demonstration in Tehran, December 1979. Such scenes were common in the early days of the Islamic Revolution, as the Ayatollah Khomeini labeled the United States "the Great Satan."

A London policeman battles a Muslim demonstrating against Salman Rushdie. In 1989 Iran's Ayatollah Khomeini issued a fatwa, or decree, calling on faithful Muslims to kill the Indian-born British author, claiming Rushdie's novel *The Satanic Verses* was blasphemous.

over other issues. In spite of opposition, the Council of Guardians quickly increased the legal list of moral offenses and strictly enforced, for example, an Islamic dress code for women. In addition, though many opposed interfering in the affairs of other peoples and countries, support flowed out of Iran for revolutionary movements in Lebanon, Saudi Arabia, Bahrain, Iraq, and the Philippines. Khomeini also issued a fatwa sentencing British author Salman Rushdie to death on the grounds that his book *The Satanic Verses* was blasphemous, which fed perceptions that Iran wanted to impose its will internationally. And after 1980 Iran developed anti-Western policies on a range of international issues; tensions remained high with the United States over the hostage crisis and with France over France's support of Iraq.

After Khomeini's death in 1989, however, President Hashemi Rafsanjani was able to restrict the power of some of the more conservative members of the Council of Guardians and implement economic reform, and during the 1990s, momentum built among younger Iranians and women for liberal reforms at the national level. In 1997 the country elected Mohammad Khatami president of Iran with over 70 percent of the vote, a result interpreted as a call for more democracy and less power for Khomeini's successor, Ali Khamenei, and the Council of Guardians.

Khatami has defended Islamic identity and values while calling for increased dialogue with the non-Muslim world, though this has not stopped him from condemning the United States for continued patterns of domination. Echoing earlier modernist reformers, Khatami has called for new connections between tradition and modernity, but without conceding any Islamic values. In 2001 Khatami asserted that Iran had adopted a democracy in accordance with religious norms; he was reelected that year with 76 percent of the vote.

Despite some reforms in the Majlis, Khatami continues to face staunch opposition from the Council of Guardians, which has silenced his backers in the press and jailed many of his supporters. Though many Iranians are disappointed that he has not been able to achieve more, Khatami maintains his belief in gradual change and continues his fight for increased democracy and conversation with the outside world. Under his guidance, Iran and the United States have resumed limited talks.

Mohammad Khatami, Iran's president, is considered a moderate by many Western observers, but his reform efforts have largely been thwarted by the country's powerful Shiite clerics.

A scene from the hajj, the annual pilgrimage of Muslims to Mecca. Because it contains Islam's holiest sites, Saudi Arabia claims a special position within the Muslim faith. But that status can be a double-edged sword: Islamic militants have condemned the Saudi monarchy for allowing "infidel" Westerners in the land of the Prophet's birth.

Saudi Arabia

Saudi Arabia was established as the first modern Islamic state in 1932, but its origins lie in the Wahhabi movement of the 1700s, when Islamic scholar Muhammad ibn Abd al-Wahhab and tribal chief Muhammad ibn Saud formed an alliance to seek power.

As the location of the holy cities of Mecca and Medina and the site of the annual hajj to Mecca, Saudi Arabia is still very important to Islamic faith and practice. The Saudi royal family and religious leaders claim that Saudi Arabia is the protector of the holy cities and of Muslim pilgrims. They further maintain that, in spite of its great oil wealth and its alliances with Western nations, the kingdom is still true to the tenets of Wahhabism.

WAHHABIS AND THE HOUSE OF SAUD

After legal training in Mecca and Medina, al-Wahhab returned
to his hometown of Najd and was appalled to find few Islamic rituals observed and superstition and tribal conflict rampant. Al-
Wahhab thought the moral decay and tribal warfare in Arabia
indicated a betrayal of Islam and a breakdown in the *umma*. He
blamed the chaos in Arabia on innovations in Islamic practice—
especially Sufi practices like the worship of saints and visits to
their tombs—and called for a return to the practices of
Muhammad and his companions. Al-Wahhab believed that all
events after Muhammad's day, including legal rulings of the
ulama, were open for review and reinterpretation based on the

Rhythmic chanting helps these Iraqi members of a Sufi order enter a religious trance. Though
the Sufi mystic tradition has a long history within Islam, some fundamentalists, such as the
highly influential Muhammad ibn Abd al-Wahhab, have denied its validity.

earliest sources of Islam. He advocated the practice of *ijtihad* (individual interpretation of the law) as the only way to rid Islam of the corrupt beliefs and practices he thought were eating away at the fabric of Islamic society.

Al-Wahhab's followers have commonly been called the Wahhabis, though at the time they called themselves the Muwahiddun (the "Unitarians" who proclaim and uphold monotheism). The Wahhabis began to destroy Sufi shrines, tombs, and holy trees, which upset local citizens so much that they drove al-Wahhab's forces out in 1744.

The Wahhabis found refuge in Diriya, where al-Wahhab developed an alliance with the House of Saud through the local tribal chief, Muhammad ibn Saud (d. 1765). They sought to unite devout Muslims under the banner of true Islam and declared holy war on any person, Muslim or otherwise, who did not join their fight. Al-Wahhab provided the spiritual foundation for their struggle, but Saud was declared imam and directed the warfare.

The Wahhabis continued destroying tombs and shrines. In 1802 they massacred the townspeople of Karbala and desecrated the tomb of Hussein (the Prophet's grandson), an action for which many Shiites have never forgiven the Wahhabis. By 1805 the Wahhabis had seized Mecca and Medina, destroying the domes over the graves of Muhammad and his companions. Under Wahhabi rule, Arabian culture changed drastically. The Wahhabis prohibited fancy dress, jewelry, and art forms such as dance and poetry.

However, the Wahhabis' control of Mecca and Medina led to an inevitable conflict with the Ottoman Empire, which saw Wahhabi rule in Arabia as a threat to the stability of the Middle East, and more particularly to the thriving pilgrimage trade in Damascus and Baghdad. Therefore, in 1812 the sultan of the empire sent forces against the Wahhabis. By 1819 the Wahhabis were thoroughly defeated and their imam, Abdullah ibn Saud, was executed. This ended the first phase of Wahhabi rule, but the alliance between the House of Saud and the Wahhabis did not end.

THE FOUNDING OF SAUDI ARABIA

After a long period of dormancy, the Saudi dynasty reemerged in 1902, when Abdul Aziz ibn Saud captured the Arabian city Riyadh and began gradually to extend his territory. Most of Ibn Saud's warriors, called the *Ikhwan* ("brotherhood"), were Bedouins. They were fierce in battle, very interested in the loot they could win in war, and confident that if they died fighting they would become martyrs and immediately go to paradise.

Ibn Saud, who saw the Arabian tribes relying on tribal law rather than Islamic law to settle their conflicts, stressed the equality of all Muslims and sought to replace tribal affiliations with loyalty to Islam—a repeat of the intervention in Arab tribal society by Muhammad ibn Saud and Muhammad ibn Abd al-Wahhab. Abdul Aziz ibn Saud asserted his authority as the descendant of both the House of Saud and al-Wahhab—the two families had intermarried extensively since their alliance was first formed more than a century before. Ibn Saud also married into the families of tribal chiefs in order to solidify his control over their tribes.

Under Ibn Saud's direction, the Wahhabis identified, and subjected to dire punishment or even death, any Muslims they deemed to have strayed from the faith by failing to follow Islamic law. They encouraged nomadic tribes to settle in colonies, where life was organized around the mosque and where they were educated in Wahhabism and observed for correct behavior.

By the early 1920s, Ibn Saud had greatly expanded his territory on the Arabian Peninsula. In 1924 he took control of Mecca, and a year later Medina also surrendered. But Ibn Saud did not completely secure his power over the Arabian Peninsula until 1929, and part of the struggle occurred from within his own ranks. The Ikhwan, now numbering 150,000, were unhappy that Ibn Saud allowed non-Wahhabi pilgrims to the holy sites, maintained a tobacco tax as a way to fill the government's coffers (they considered smoking against Islamic law), and used modern technology. The zeal of the Wahhabis also proved problematic for Ibn Saud;

Abdul Aziz ibn Saud, founder of the Kingdom of Saudi Arabia.

they wanted to move beyond the peninsula to continue to defeat unbelievers and spread Wahhabi beliefs, while he sought to implement fixed national borders and thus gain recognition from foreign powers for his new nation.

With the help of the British, Ibn Saud finally assembled a separate army and defeated the Ikhwan. Thus, the political arm of the Wahhab-Saud alliance won out, and the purely spiritual war waged by the Wahhabis was over. In September 1932, Abdul Aziz ibn Saud declared himself king and named the new nation the Kingdom of Saudi Arabia. While he had thwarted the Wahhabi drive to conquer territory beyond Saudi Arabia, Ibn Saud remained true to the alliance by putting the crossed swords of al-Wahhab and the House of Saud on the country's new flag.

THE SAUDI MONARCHY AND THE ENFORCEMENT OF ISLAMIC LAW

Under Ibn Saud, the House of Saud unified the tribal cultures of Arabia and become the first modern Islamic state. Ibn Saud emphasized his role as keeper of the holy cities of Mecca and Medina and as protector of all pilgrims making the annual hajj to Mecca. He assumed power as the head of the government, the commander of the armed forces, and the chief over all Arabian tribes. He also declared that the position of leader would be passed down through his family.

Ibn Saud stipulated the Qur'an as Saudi Arabia's constitution. He said an advisory assembly made up of *ulama* and lay business and community leaders would form to advise him on matters of governance, but he never established this council. In 1960 a new national constitution was proposed to Abdul Aziz ibn Saud's successor, King Saud ibn Saud. It would declare Islam the state religion, affirm the right to private property and capital, and create a national legislative assembly, two-thirds of which would be popularly elected. Saud rejected the proposal, citing the Qur'an as the only constitution Saudi Arabia would ever need.

In 1962, after the Islamic monarch of North Yemen was overthrown in a popular uprising, King Saud and his brother Faisal ibn Saud feared a similar rebellion in Saudi Arabia. To forestall this, they promised economic development and a new constitution based on the Qur'an and the Hadith that would guarantee basic rights to all citizens, including some freedom of expression. They also promised a judicial council to reinterpret the Sharia in light of the problems presented by modern society. The council was not formed until 1975, however, and constitutional reforms finally enacted by King Fahd in 1992 still stipulated the Qur'an and the Hadith as the constitution of Saudi Arabia and did not make any provisions for freedom of speech. A new advisory assembly was also formed in 1992, but the king appointed its members.

The enforcement of Islamic behavior in Saudi Arabia is conducted locally through the mosque leader (imam), the *ulama*, religious judges (*qadi*), and the religious police (*muttawin*). The *muttawin* make sure all citizens comply with Islamic law and practices and provide instruction on how to follow Islamic legal rulings. They see to it that businesses close during prayer times, no one consumes alcohol, and no one breaks the Ramadan ban on food and drink from sunrise to sunset. Worship is also monitored; any speeches given in a mosque must be pre-approved. Women must wear Islamic dress (a loose black cloak called an *abaya* and a headscarf called a *hijab*) while in public, and they can't leave the house alone or drive.

The national minister of religion and justice, traditionally a descendant of al-Wahhab himself, advises the king, as does the chief *qadi*. The judiciary branch is made up entirely of *ulama*, who rely solely on the Sharia. The courts rule on matters of family and property law. The death penalty is mandatory—and usually applied quickly—for adultery, murder, robbery that involves violence, drug violations, and **apostasy**, and it is sometimes decreed for those who exercise freedom of speech.

However, while the *ulama* follow the Hanbali school of Sunni Islamic law and apply it very strictly where specific laws exist, they rule more liberally on other matters. Thus, although women face many restrictions in their daily lives, they are allowed education through the university level, and many hold professional jobs. And while the Wahhabis and some of the *ulama* declared modern technology like phones, cars, airplanes, and television unacceptable Western innovations, the monarchy has persisted and gained acceptance for their use.

RELATIONSHIP WITH THE WORLD

A dual allegiance to the West and to Arab countries has consistently complicated Saudi Arabia's foreign affairs, a situation created in part by the 1938 discovery of oil in Saudi Arabia under King Abdul Aziz ibn Saud. From the beginning of oil exploration, American and European technicians and engineers came to work in the kingdom, a fact condemned by Wahhabist leaders.

By 1950 the Arabian-American Oil Company (Aramco) was generating vast wealth from oil sales, primarily in the West. King Saud fostered his country's relationship with the United States, allowing

Saudi Arabia has about one-quarter of the world's proven reserves of petroleum. While oil has brought incredible wealth into the kingdom, it has also brought Western influences—a situation condemned by Saudi Arabia's conservative Wahhabi Muslims.

American forces use of an air base in Dhahran and purchasing significant quantities of U.S. arms. The sons of wealthy families were also sent to study at U.S. universities. As interaction with the West increased, however, the *ulama* and the monarchy joined the Wahhabists in worrying about excessive Western influence.

King Saud's half-brother Faisal became king in 1964. He was a pious favorite of the *ulama* who claimed maternal lineage from al-Wahhab. Under King Faisal, the Saudi government refused to renew the U.S. lease on the Dhahran base in 1962. In 1967 Faisal enacted a series of reforms that imposed stricter dress codes for women and children and enforced prayer times for government employees. The king led the 1973–74 Organization of Petroleum Exporting Countries (OPEC) oil embargo on the nations that supported Israel in its 1973 war with Egypt and Syria. The embargo resulted in a spike in worldwide oil prices, and the increased revenues that flowed into Saudi Arabia as a result enabled Faisal to improve his country's transportation, education, and health care systems.

However, Faisal was unwilling to adopt policies that were completely anti-Western. In 1971 Saudi Arabia and five other Persian Gulf countries signed a new agreement with Western oil companies. By the mid-1970s, the number of American civilian and military personnel working in Saudi Arabia had increased dramatically, and many members of the government openly flirted with American values and lifestyles. Wealthy Arab businessmen and princes, it was rumored, engaged in all kinds of Western vices—drinking, gambling, adultery—in their palaces and abroad.

In March 1975, Faisal was assassinated by a nephew and succeeded by Khalid ibn Abdul Aziz. The Saudi government struggled to keep up with the fast pace of development brought on by the oil economy and mass migrations to the cities. The revolution in Iran in 1979 deeply alarmed the monarchy, especially since the Iranian media repeatedly accused the House of Saud of corrupt behavior. King Khalid responded by cracking down on practices that could be considered un-Islamic and publicly punishing royals who broke the law. Then, in late 1979, 400 armed Wahhabist militants, distressed by what they saw as the materialism of the Saudi rulers, seized Islam's holiest shrine, the Grand Mosque in Mecca, and issued demands for changes. Although the government retook the mosque and executed the rebels, this event heightened awareness of the Saudi government's vulnerability to both external and internal threats.

INCREASING FUNDAMENTALIST OPPOSITION

Khalid died in June 1982 and was succeeded by Fahd, who sought to maintain traditional Islamic values while continuing the process of rapid modernization. He stressed his role as the custodian of Islam's holiest sites to try to shield the pro-West Saudi regime from opposition by Islamic militants. In 1987, however, more than 400 people were killed when Saudi police clashed with Iranian hajj pilgrims. Relations between Saudi Arabia and Iran deteriorated, and Iranian pilgrims boycotted the hajj for several years.

Fundamentalist opposition to the Saudi regime increased

The ruins of the Khobar Towers housing complex near Dhahran, Saudi Arabia, where in 1996 a truck bomb claimed the lives of 19 U.S. Air Force personnel. The United States later indicted 14 members of the militant Islamic organization Hizbollah in the attack; 13 were Saudis.

through the 1990s. After Iraq invaded Kuwait in 1990, the Saudi government allowed hundreds of thousands of U.S.-led coalition troops to deploy on its territory, which opposition leaders denounced as a violation of sacred Islamic territory. Nevertheless, U.S. forces remained stationed in Saudi Arabia for more than a decade. In 1994 the Saudi government cracked down on fundamentalist clergy and scholars and established the Higher Council for Islamic Affairs to curb fundamentalist tendencies among the *ulama*.

Terrorist incidents on Saudi soil in the 1990s illustrated the level of militant frustration with the Saudi government's ties to the West, and the United States in particular. In 1995 a car bomb killed seven people, including five Americans, at the offices of the Saudi National Guard in Riyadh. In 1996 a bomb exploded at the Khobar Towers housing complex for U.S. military personnel near Dhahran, killing 19 U.S. soldiers and wounding 300 others. Threats against military personnel were made in subsequent years, and in 2003, as the U.S. military was pulling out of the country, three foreign residential compounds in Riyadh were hit by suicide bombings, killing 35. Among the dead were Americans, Europeans, and Saudis; it was the first time terrorists had targeted civilians, including women and children, in Saudi Arabia.

Critics of close U.S.-Saudi relations point to the fact that, though the Saudi government has officially denounced terrorism, many Saudi individuals and charities have used the kingdom's great wealth to spread Wahhabi-style fundamentalist thought throughout the Islamic world. By gaining extensive control of printing presses in the Middle East, these fundamentalists have ensured a pro-Wahhabi bent in publications, and they have established schools and mosques throughout the Islamic world to teach fundamentalist Wahhabi doctrine. Today, Saudi individuals and charities routinely fund militant groups in the Philippines, Chechnya, the Balkans, Egypt, and Somalia, among other places. Links have also been alleged between Saudi sources and the terrorist organizations Hamas and al-Qaeda.

Bin Laden: Saudi Dissident

Saudi Arabia's relationship with one of its own former citizens, Osama bin Laden, has greatly complicated the international discussion of Islamic militant activities and terrorism against the Western world.

The son of a wealthy Saudi businessman, Osama bin Laden was born in 1957 and grew up in a world of privilege that included close ties with the Saudi royal family. His father ran a strict Islamic household. As a college student, bin Laden was increasingly influenced by Wahhabism, an Islamic scholar named Abdallah Azzam who was later an influential figure in the war in Afghanistan, the writings of Sayyid Qutb, and opposition movements against the Saudi regime.

In 1979 bin Laden went to Peshawar, Pakistan, to join other Arabs training to fight the Soviet occupation in Afghanistan. He provided funding for facilities in Peshawar and by 1986 was commanding Arab forces in battle in Afghanistan. It was there that he founded al-Qaeda ("the Base") to manage the flow of Arab fighters into battle; he also interacted with American CIA operatives giving support to the Afghan resistance.

By the time Iraq invaded Kuwait in 1990, bin Laden was back in Saudi Arabia working in his father's business. He offered his services as a trained fighter to the Saudi royalty, only to discover that U.S. forces were to be stationed in his home country. This, more than any other event, shaped bin Laden's outlook, for he could not accept Western soldiers in Islam's birthplace. He increasingly condemned the Saudi government as corrupt and went into exile in 1992, first in Afghanistan and then in the Islamic Republic of Sudan, where he allegedly founded a training center for terrorists. Saudi Arabia stripped him of his citizenship in 1994. Bin Laden was suspected of involvement in two anti-American incidents that took place in 1993: the bombing of the World Trade Center and the killing of U.S. troops during a battle in Mogadishu, Somalia. Under U.S. pressure, Sudan expelled him

Osama bin Laden, whose al-Qaeda network is blamed for much anti-U.S. terrorism—including the September 11, 2001, attacks on the World Trade Center and Pentagon—is also a bitter opponent of Saudi Arabia's ruling family.

in 1996. Back in Afghanistan, under the protection of that nation's fundamentalist Islamic Taliban government, bin Laden increased his base of operations; the United States later accused him of backing the bombings of the American embassies in Kenya and Tanzania in 1998 and the USS *Cole* in Yemen in 2000.

With his Wahhabist worldview, bin Laden condemns Westerners as un-Islamic and says they are subject to violent jihad. In addition to denouncing the presence of U.S. troops in Saudi Arabia, he has accused the United States of extending its influence in the Arab world merely to protect its access to oil, supporting authoritarian Arab governments, oppressing Palestinians by backing Israel unconditionally, and killing millions of Iraqis through U.N. economic sanctions against Saddam Hussein.

The September 11, 2001, attacks on the United States complicated the relationship between Saudi Arabia and the United States. All 19 of the hijackers had ties to al-Qaeda, and 15 were Saudi citizens. Crown Prince Abdullah, Saudi Arabia's ruler, immediately condemned the attacks, but he subsequently refused to allow the United States use of Saudi facilities in its international war on terrorism, and specifically its campaigns in Afghanistan and Iraq. In 2003 the United States transferred all but a few hundred U.S. troops from Saudi Arabia to neighboring Qatar.

In Egypt—as in some other Arab countries with secular governments—social problems such as rapid population growth and high poverty rates, combined with an absence of political freedoms, have led to widespread discontent and fostered a renewed Islamic identity among many citizens.

The Arab World

The Arab world includes areas of both the Middle East and North Africa. Most Arabs do have considerable linguistic and cultural connection to the peoples of Arabia, but some are considered Arab only because their lands were conquered during eras of Arab expansion. Arab countries in the Middle East include Bahrain, Iraq, Jordan, Kuwait, Lebanon, Oman, Qatar, Saudi Arabia, Syria, the United Arab Emirates, and Yemen. Arab countries in North Africa include Algeria, Djibouti, Egypt, Libya, Mauritania, Morocco, Somalia, Sudan, and Tunisia.

Islamic fundamentalism has deep roots in the Arab region. The predominantly Muslim countries of the region have been at the center of conflict between the Islamic and secular modern worldviews for several reasons: the central Middle East was the site of some of the greatest Western colonial expansion, the West backed the founding of Israel, and colonialism and its aftermath brought severe economic and educational impoverishment and brutal political repression to the region. As Arab countries have experienced rapid change and severe social problems, many Muslims have found a renewed sense of identity by returning to their faith.

Together with a Pan-Arab consciousness, which promotes the interests of Arabs in general, Islamic fundamentalism has dominated political life in the Arab world since the late 1800s. Since the 1970s, however, as secular nationalism has faltered, Islamic fundamentalism has increasingly replaced the Pan-Arab movement by promising to cleanse the region of foreign influences and provide political and economic stability through the application of Islamic principles.

Two central factors, the birth of Israel and the discovery of oil, have shaped the history of the Arab world in the last century. *Ideological* and military conflicts over these two developments have opened the way for fundamentalism to grow in strength and influence.

ISRAEL

As the Ottoman Empire was crumbling in the mid-1800s, European powers increasingly encroached on Arab countries in search of raw materials, markets, military bases, and colonies. Western ideas led to widespread modernization and eventually fostered Arab nationalism, but Europeans held the financial and political power. British and French leaders promised independence to Arabs if they resisted the Ottoman Empire in World War I, but they later broke their promise and divided the empire between them. The abolition of the caliphate in 1924 was also a severe blow, for Muslims had long sustained the idea of one global Islamic community (the *umma*).

British and French influence in the Middle East waned after

World War II (1939–1945), as a succession of Arab nations won their independence. Arab identity was at issue as Arab countries fought off European control, and as the leaders of six independent Arab nations formed the League of Arab States in 1945 (the organization's membership subsequently grew to 22 states).

Arab solidarity would be seriously tested, and relations with Western powers severely strained, in the aftermath of the creation of Israel in 1948. More than half a century later, Israel (along with the plight of Palestinians under the control of the Jewish state) remains at the center of Arab, and Islamic fundamentalist, concerns.

Modern Jewish aspirations for a homeland in Palestine may be traced to the 1890s, with the founding of the Zionist movement. Zionism may be defined as Jewish territorial nationalism. During World War I, Great Britain issued the Balfour Declaration, by which it promised to facilitate the establishment of "a national home for the Jewish people" in Palestine, though it was emphasized that "nothing shall be done which may prejudice the civil and religious rights of existing non-Jewish communities" there. Under a mandate from the League of Nations, Britain took over the administration of Palestine, formerly part of the Ottoman Empire, after the war's conclusion. During the 1920s, as Jewish immigration to the area increased, violent clashes between Jewish settlers and Arab Palestinians erupted. Violence between the two communities continued through the 1930s. In 1936 Palestinians rose up against British rule and battled Jewish forces in a revolt that was finally suppressed in 1939, on the eve of World War II.

Unrest in Palestine only intensified after World War II, and Britain ultimately decided to turn over the issue of what to do with Palestine to the newly formed United Nations. In November 1947 the U.N. approved a plan to partition Palestine into a Palestinian Arab state and a Jewish state. The Arab nations made it clear that they would not accept a Jewish state.

On May 14, 1948, when Britain officially withdrew from Palestine and Israel declared its independence, the armies of Arab League members Egypt, Transjordan (later Jordan), Iraq, Syria, and

Lebanon, as promised, moved to crush the new Jewish state. In the ensuing war, however, Israel not only defeated all its Arab enemies but also gained significantly more territory than had been allotted it under the U.N. partition plan. For the Palestinians, the war was a catastrophe. By the time the fighting ended in January 1949, about 750,000 had been uprooted from their homes, and the Palestinian state envisioned in the U.N. partition plan was gone. Israel had conquered some of the territory; Egypt had taken Gaza, along the Mediterranean coast; and Jordan occupied the West Bank.

Over the following decades, Arab-Israeli relations remained abysmal. The Arab countries refused to recognize Israel's right to exist, and skirmishes between Israel and its neighbors erupted periodically. In 1956 Israel defeated Egypt during the Suez War, capturing most of the Sinai Peninsula but later returning the territory at the insistence of the United States. Following an Arab conference in Cairo, Egypt, in 1964, the Palestine Liberation Organization (PLO) was formed. Its mission was to unify Palestinian efforts to "liberate" Palestine from Israel, and funding came from various Arab governments.

The Six-Day War, fought in June 1967, was a watershed in the Arab-Israeli conflict. As Egypt, Syria, and Jordan were preparing to attack the Jewish state, Israel struck first. In less than a week, Israel smashed the combined armed forces of its enemies. The decisive defeat struck a devastating blow to Arab confidence; Israel clearly was the region's preeminent military power. (Arab critics charged that this was due largely to the military aid Israel received from the West, especially the United States.) As a result of the Six-Day War, Israel also took control of additional territory: Gaza and most of the Sinai Peninsula, which had belonged to Egypt; Syria's Golan Heights; and the West Bank, which Jordan had claimed since 1948. Most significantly, this brought several million Palestinians in Gaza and the West Bank under Israeli military occupation, a situation that, over the following decades, would breed more Palestinian and Arab resentment and lead to much bloodshed.

After another war with Israel in October 1973, Egyptian president Anwar Sadat traveled to Jerusalem in 1977 to address Israel's parliament, the Knesset. Sadat announced his desire for peace, and that opening led to the Camp David Accords of 1978, a framework for peace negotiated with mediation from U.S. president Jimmy Carter. The following year, Israel and Egypt concluded an official peace treaty, under the terms of which Egypt officially recognized Israel (becoming the first Arab nation to do so), and Israel returned the Sinai Peninsula to Egypt.

Sadat's peace agreement with Israel provoked outrage throughout the Arab world, leading to Egypt's expulsion from the Arab League. And, although the Camp David Accords had envisioned a peaceful settlement to the Israeli-Palestinian conflict that might include an independent Palestinian state in the West Bank and Gaza, neither the Arab nations nor the PLO supported such a course. Palestinian grievances against Israel—including ongoing Jewish settlement of the West Bank and Gaza Strip—continued to fester, and in December 1987 a violent Palestinian uprising known as the *intifada* ("shaking off") broke out in the occupied territories.

An Israeli army convoy rolls across Egypt's Sinai Peninsula during the Six-Day War. The June 1967 conflict brought Israel a stunning military victory and important territorial gains—along with the quandary of how to govern several million Palestinians now under its control.

After several years of almost daily bloodshed, Israel and the PLO began conducting secret negotiations, which culminated in 1993 in the Oslo Accords. That agreement, essentially a land-for-peace deal, called for an Israeli military pullback from most of the occupied territories, a five-year period of security cooperation and limited Palestinian self-rule, and then final-status negotiations to settle outstanding issues and fix the borders of the Palestinian state.

The Oslo Accords paved the way for an Israel-Jordan peace treaty, as well as better Israeli relations with such Arab countries as Qatar, Morocco, and Tunisia. Unfortunately, while a Palestinian governing authority was set up in the West Bank and Gaza under the leadership of PLO chairman Yasir Arafat, the peace process unraveled well before the final-status talks the Oslo Accords had envisioned. A second *intifada*, which broke out in September 2000, effectively ended the Oslo Accords and ushered in a long cycle of Palestinian terrorism and Israeli retaliation. By early 2003, the *intifada* had claimed the lives of some 2,000

The Camp David Accords marked the first time an Arab nation had made peace with Israel. Seen here celebrating the breakthrough are (from left) President Anwar Sadat of Egypt; U.S. president Jimmy Carter, who helped mediate the agreement; and Menachem Begin, prime minister of Israel.

Palestinians and 700 Israelis. Throughout, Arabs have charged that the United States blindly supports Israel and what they view as its oppression of the Palestinian people. Israel and the United States, in turn, accuse the Palestinian Authority of doing nothing to stop suicide bombings committed against Israelis by Arab-supported fundamentalist groups such as Hamas and Islamic Jihad. Though statehood for the Palestinians remains a central goal of many Arabs and Islamic fundamentalists, when—or even if—that goal might be achieved remains uncertain.

Oil

The second major factor that has shaped the contemporary Arab world, after Israel, is oil. Together with Iran, the Middle East has about two-thirds of the world's total known petroleum reserves; Saudi Arabia alone claims about one-quarter of all proven reserves. Oil was first discovered in the Persian Gulf during the 1920s, and since then Western powers have been keenly interested in the region. The strategic importance of the Middle East and its oil also attracted the involvement and intervention of the post–World War II superpowers, the United States and the Soviet Union. After the Suez War between Israel and Egypt in 1956, the Soviet Union allied itself with the nationalist leadership of Egypt, Iraq, and Syria, while the United States continued to side with Israel and formed close relationships with the Jordanian and Saudi Arabian monarchies. For many decades, the Cold War between the United States and the Soviet Union fueled much of the conflict in the Middle East. With the fall of the Soviet Union, however, former Russian allies had no choice but to deal with the United States as the lone superpower.

The Arab oil-producing states formed the Organization of Petroleum Exporting Countries (OPEC) in 1960. In support of Egypt in the 1973 October War with Israel, OPEC instituted steep price hikes for its crude oil, which further raised U.S. concerns about the security of the oil supply. Since then, U.S. strategists have

Two female members of the al-Aqsa Martyrs Brigade, an extremist Palestinian group that has carried out suicide bombing attacks against Israelis.

sought to build a troop presence in the Persian Gulf to ensure the flow of oil in the region. American troops were called into action in the Persian Gulf twice over a dozen-year period. In the Gulf War of 1991, the United States led an international coalition that expelled Iraq from Kuwait, which Iraq had invaded the previous year. In 2003 U.S. forces invaded Iraq and toppled the regime of Saddam Hussein, an action President George W. Bush framed as part of the U.S. "war on terror"; Iraq was said to possess chemical and biological weapons in violation of its obligations under the Gulf War armistice agreement.

In each conflict with Iraq, however, Arab critics (both fundamentalists and others) complained that the main U.S. interest was to protect the flow of oil to American consumers. They condemned U.S. protection of oil resources in the Middle East as Western imperialism, and some even asserted that the United States manufactured both conflicts as pretexts for gaining more control over Arab oil fields. After the Gulf War of 1991, the United Nations imposed economic sanctions on Iraq in order to compel Saddam Hussein to comply with disarmament obligations. Those sanctions remained in effect for more than a decade, and during that time ordinary Iraqis suffered substantial increases in poverty, illness, and child mortality rates. Many Arabs charged that the United States, the staunchest backer of the sanctions, was interested only in keeping its oil supply secure and did not care about Muslim lives. Further evidence of this, the critics charged, was the slowness with which the United States responded to Serbian atrocities against Muslims during the war in Bosnia in the early 1990s.

THE NATIONALISTS AND FUNDAMENTALISTS

The birth of Israel inspired the growth of Arab nationalism. Radical army officers took over Egypt, Iraq, and Syria and vowed to destroy Israel, maintain independence from foreign influence, and develop strong economies. Though they accepted aid primarily from the Soviet Union, they sought complete sovereignty, established Western-style political patterns (parliaments, political parties, constitutions), and adopted Western legal codes. They attempted to develop modern industrial economies using the latest agricultural, transportation, and communication methods. They also accepted Western styles of art, music, and literature and Western ideas about women's rights.

However, these governments concentrated on military defense and often badly mismanaged resources. Meanwhile, migration to urban centers grew as people looked for jobs, and the gap between the rich and poor increased. The result was unrest and increasingly repressive government policies. The monarchies of Jordan and Saudi Arabia adopted similarly repressive measures to stifle calls for change in their own countries.

Radical nationalism reached its zenith in the 1960s, when Egyptian president Gamal Abdel Nasser and the Baath Party leaders of Iraq and Syria advocated Arab revolutions and socialism. However, military defeats at the hands of Israel and the 1991 collapse of the Soviet Union dealt serious blows to Arab nationalism.

It is no accident that Islamic fundamentalism in the Arab world surged precisely as nationalism began to founder, for it was by pointing both within (at the failures of nationalism and the un-Islamic ways of government leaders) and without (at the corrupting influence of foreign powers) that fundamentalist leaders persuaded Muslims to return to the fundamentals of their faith. This has resulted in opposition movements in numerous Arab countries, including Egypt, Lebanon, and Syria. It has also influenced leaders who had previously relied on secular nationalism alone to embrace Islamic principles in an effort to boost their legitimacy, as has been the case in Egypt, Iraq, Libya, Sudan, and Syria.

An important turning point was the 1967 Six-Day War with Israel. For Arabs the rapid and total defeat of the combined forces of Egypt, Syria, and Jordan was made even worse because the Israelis captured East Jerusalem and made the unified city their capital. The third-holiest city in Islam, Jerusalem plays an important role in Muslim identity. The Six-Day War starkly illustrated the flaws in the nationalist policies of Arab countries, and particularly the Egyptian brand of socialism. Arab Muslims had won the end of colonial rule, but their societies were caught in a downward spiral of decline. In response, fundamentalists cited the glorious early expansion under Muhammad and the growth of Islamic empires to illustrate that Muslim prosperity depended on being faithful to God in all matters. The current state of affairs in the Arab world, they argued, was the sign of Muslims' disobedience.

This call for religious reform tapped into new sources of pride after Egypt used Islamic symbols and language to motivate its forces to win some battles against Israel in the 1973 October War and OPEC staged its oil embargo later that year. These successes underlined the fundamentalists' message that faithfulness to God would bring new prosperity to Muslim nations. In turn, the wealthy oil nations pumped their petrodollars into Islamic organizations and movements. Finally, though it occurred in a non-Arab country, the Iranian revolution of 1979 further strengthened the claim that following the straight path of Islam would invigorate Muslim movements and lead to freedom from foreign domination.

The fundamentalist response has taken many forms to influence Arab governments in the last 20 years. Most Arab countries have an ongoing fundamentalist presence. In Egypt, Jordan, Lebanon, Kuwait, and Yemen, fundamentalist organizations have run educational and social programs, developed opposition political parties, and even occupied government positions. But militant groups have also proliferated throughout the Arab world, opposing leaders they see as un-Islamic and in turn being repressed by the government. In the Arab-Israeli conflict, the group Hamas has become a major critic of the secular Palestinian Authority.

To understand in more depth the role of fundamentalism in the Arab world today, it is instructive to closely examine three countries where fundamentalism has had different effects: Egypt, Lebanon, and Sudan. A closer look at the group Hamas also gives insight into the Arab-Israeli conflict and Arab militant responses.

EGYPT

Egypt's story can be told through the relationship between three different national governments and a diverse set of moderate and militant fundamentalist groups.

After Gamal Abdel Nasser became president in 1952, he kept Egypt on its secular nationalist path, ignoring the Muslim Brotherhood. Within just a few years, however, their opposition led him to incorporate Islamic symbols and language into his Pan-Arab socialist message in order to gain legitimacy in Islamic terms. But the Brotherhood saw Nasser's use of Islam as antithetical to a true Islamic state. After extremist members of the Brotherhood led an assassination attempt on Nasser in 1954, he brutally suppressed the organization. A second attempt by Muslim Brothers to overthrow the Nasser regime in 1965 led to the execution of Sayyid Qutb that same year.

After Nasser's death in 1970, President Anwar Sadat began to enact more pro-Western policies. He built mosques and used Islamic symbols and language to bolster his political authority. In spite of Egypt's successes against Israel in the 1973 October War, Sadat moved even closer to the West by participating in the Camp

Like his predecessors Anwar Sadat and Gamal Abdel Nasser, Egyptian president Hosni Mubarak resorted to harsh measures to suppress Islamic fundamentalists.

David Accords and supporting the shah of Iran. In order to create a counterweight to Nasserists and leftists, Sadat allowed the Muslim Brotherhood to re-form. Soon, however, the Brotherhood turned against Sadat. Joined by new student groups, the Brotherhood publicly criticized Sadat's relations with the United States and Egypt's peace treaty with Israel.

More radical groups also appeared. Some, founded by former members of the Muslim Brotherhood, believed that Brotherhood leaders had grown lax in their condemnation of Sadat. They accused Sadat of cynically using Islam for political purposes, and they believed Egypt's leaders were tools of foreign domination. These groups called for the violent overthrow of the government. They also wanted to eliminate Western cultural influences, and among their targets for attack were nightclubs and tourist hotels.

As militant groups increasingly called for armed struggle against Egyptian leaders, Sadat insisted that religion and politics must remain separate. In 1981 he ordered a crackdown in which more than 1,500 Egyptians were jailed for opposition activities. Later that year, members of the militant group Tanzim al-Jihad ("Jihad Organization") assassinated the Egyptian president, claiming his pro-West policies made him a corrupt "pharaoh."

When Hosni Mubarak succeeded Sadat as president, he created a more open atmosphere. He quickly put down militant actions, but he also allowed a measure of free speech in media outlets, and a number of fundamentalist leaders thus gained a wider audience. Fundamentalists began to develop a broader base, fostering renewed religious practices and offering social services in areas like education, banking, and housing.

By the late 1980s, however, Egyptians' increased involvement in Islamic organizations and the government's inability to create economic opportunities for its citizens led to renewed volatility. Mubarak was unhappy with the broad fundamentalist effect on the population. Militant groups assassinated government officials and attacked foreigners, and by the 1990s Mubarak increasingly used authoritarian tactics to suppress all fundamentalist groups, including both the Muslim Brotherhood and the militants. The Brotherhood had become the main opposition in parliamentary elections, but Mubarak shut down their resistance by jailing their key leaders. He also took control of all independent mosques, many of which had been highly critical of his government.

With a burgeoning population and mass migration to its cities, Egypt's social problems continue to grow. Fundamentalist assessments of the government are widespread among Egyptians, but the Mubarak regime has suppressed both militant and moderate opposition groups and shut out public debate. Many Egyptians continue to be dismayed by Mubarak's friendly relations with the United States and were deeply angered when Mubarak blamed Saddam Hussein rather than the United States for the invasion of Iraq in 2003.

LEBANON

Lebanon provides perhaps the prime example of how the Iranian revolution has directly affected the Islamic politics of Arab countries.

The French oversaw the creation of Lebanon after the breakup of the Ottoman Empire, and it developed into a stable, Westernized country with a government that reflected its diverse religious communities, including Christians, Sunnis, Shiites, and **Druze**. Political offices and government jobs were allotted according to the various groups' proportions in the Lebanese population as counted by the 1932 census. As the largest group, Christians were guaranteed to remain the dominant political power. However, as the Ayatollah Khomeini was becoming the leader of Iranian Shiites in the 1970s, Iranian-born cleric Musa Sadr was organizing Shiites in Lebanon to demand that the national government reflect the country's changing demographic makeup: by this time Shiites had in fact replaced Christians as the largest group. He emphasized the historical Shiite battle for the dispossessed and organized the Movement of the Disinherited to protest economic inequality and the Israeli military threat in south

Lebanon. Out of this group evolved Amal, the militant arm of Sadr's movement.

Amal attracted more followers after Israel invaded Lebanon in 1978 and 1982, and Sadr disappeared in Libya in 1978 and became revered as a Shiite martyr. But Amal's moderate policies in subsequent years—seeking full Shiite participation in a pluralistic government and carefully avoiding any calls for an Islamic state—angered young militants, who formed their own groups. Among the most radical of these was Hizbollah ("Party of God"), which held up Iran's ruling religious authorities as a model, condemned foreign imperialism, and called for a Lebanese Islamic state. Iranian money flowed into Lebanon to fund Hizbollah, and Shiite mosques became the group's centers of organization. In the early 1980s Hizbollah allied itself with other militant groups to fight in

A sniper of the Shiite Amal militia scans an intersection in West Beirut, circa 1984. Lebanon's 15-year civil war devastated the once-prosperous country.

Lebanon's civil war (1975–1990) and conducted terrorist activities, including bombings at the American and French embassies and at the barracks of international (mostly American) peacekeeping forces in 1983.

After the civil war ended in 1990, Hizbollah joined Amal in helping rebuild Lebanon and participating in national elections. It did not, however, stop fighting the Israeli occupation in southern Lebanon and continued to occupy a border zone there after Israel pulled out in 2000. Iran has more recently made gestures to curb Hizbollah's militant activities in southern Lebanon, as part of increasing diplomacy with the United States.

SUDAN

Sudan offers a key example of the long history of fundamentalism in Arabized northern Africa.

In 1881 Muhammad Ahmad ibn Abdallah declared himself the Mahdi and led a rebellion that expelled the Ottoman rulers. He installed an Islamic state and banned many activities, including the use of tobacco, marriage feasts, and Sufi practices such as processions and visits to saints' tombs. British forces defeated the Mahdists in 1898, but Muslim leaders did not give up on an Islamic state; by the 1930s, nationalist and Islamic factions were insisting on independence and vying for power. Following Sudan's full independence in 1956, a series of civilian and military governments presided over regional conflicts and a devastated economy.

As Sudan gained its full independence, some national leaders pushed for Westernization, while the powerful Islamic cleric Hassan al-Tourabi called for a process of modernization only through Islamic principles. But the development of an Islamic state was hindered by internal conflict. As a result of British rule, national power was consolidated in the north, while minority populations in the south were disenfranchised. In 1955 southerners began a revolt that lasted until the early 1970s and resumed in

1983. Some observers have framed the civil war as a conflict between Muslims and Christians. In reality, while Sunni Muslims make up 70 percent of the population, Christians make up only 5 percent, and the rest of the Sudanese (25 percent) hold *indigenous* beliefs. While the conflict is in part based on religion, it is in many ways a battle between the Muslims who have power and those who don't. As in much of Africa, ethnic divisions are also important; Sudan is home to 19 major ethnic groups who speak a total of 150 different languages.

In the 1960s and 1970s, the primary fundamentalist Islamic response to the conflict came from the National Islamic Front (NIF), under al-Tourabi's direction. In 1983 the newly elected prime minister Muhammad Gaafur al-Nimeiry instituted strict Islamic law and reformed the judicial system. Alcohol and gambling were forbidden, and theft, adultery, murder, and related offenses were judged according to the Sharia. Non-Muslims were exempt from Sharia penalties except when convicted of murder or theft. Nimeiry also declared Arabic the official language of the educational system, which further fueled the conflict between the Khartoum government and the southern-based Sudan People's Liberation Movement (SPLM).

In 1989 Omar Ahmed al-Bashir led a military coup against the government and, under al-Tourabi's guidance, reinforced Islamic law. The NIF took over the government and the military and silenced political opponents. In 1992 the army mounted an offensive against the SPLM, but the civil war continued. By 2003 the civil war had resulted in the deaths of an estimated 1.5 million Sudanese and turned an additional 4 million into refugees.

Amid accusations that the NIF has committed war crimes and revived slavery, al-Bashir was elected president again in 1997, and al-Tourabi switched strategies, moving from behind the scenes to win election to the national assembly. Al-Bashir has promised democracy, while al-Tourabi has begun a new party that is less conservative in its interpretation of Islam and more practical in its pursuit of political goals. The application of Sharia has since grown more flexible. The Khartoum government and the SPLM finally signed a ceasefire agreement in 2002.

HAMAS

By 1945 the Muslim Brotherhood had established branches in Palestine. Most Palestinians, however, were attracted to secular nationalist organizations, including the guerrilla groups that joined in 1964 to form the PLO. But during the first *intifada*, Islamism gained new adherents among Palestinians who became disillusioned with the seeming inability of the secular Palestinian leadership to make gains against the Israelis. In 1987 the Brotherhood founded the militant Islamic group Hamas ("fervor"), which soon became the primary alternative to the PLO. The

A Hamas rally in the Gaza Strip, December 2003. The coffin is meant to symbolize the death of the Israeli-Palestinian peace process.

Brotherhood's grassroots organization gave Hamas the structure it needed to grow quickly, appealing to older Palestinians with its message of Islamic reform and to angry Palestinian youth with its methods of jihad.

Hamas emphasizes the Islamic practices of prayer, fasting, and proper behavior as essential to a successful battle against Israeli occupation. The group views the Arab-Israeli conflict as a religious struggle between Islam and Judaism, unlike the PLO, which sees it as an issue of statehood and individual rights. Hamas has built a wide network of social services, political education, and community leadership. During the late 1980s and 1990s, its popularity grew with each failure of the PLO to achieve real progress toward peace.

In 1992 some Hamas subgroups also began participating in guerrilla warfare against Israeli forces. And in 1994, after an Israeli shot and killed 29 Muslims worshipping in a Hebron mosque, Hamas began suicide bombings. Over the next decade, dozens of these attacks would kill and maim Israeli civilians in markets, on buses, and in other public places, often provoking harsh Israeli crackdowns in the West Bank or Gaza Strip. The Palestinians who carry out these attacks (typically young men or women in their late teens or twenties), as well as the leaders who recruit them, reject the label "suicide bomber." Suicide is prohibited in Islamic law, and militant Hamas members who blow themselves and Israelis up believe they are simply sacrificing themselves for the cause and will be greatly rewarded in paradise. Thus they favor the term *martyr*.

While Hamas leaders and other Islamic authorities have defended the killing of Israeli civilians, the tactic has caused dismay among other Muslims, who say that violence against noncombatants tarnishes the image of Islam on the global stage. The United States has condemned Hamas as a terrorist organization, but the militant members of Hamas continue their bombings and their call for the complete withdrawal of Israelis from all Palestinian territory.

Indonesian Muslim youths perform traditional music. Nearly 9 in 10 Indonesians are followers of Islam, and in recent years the secular government has faced increasing challenges from fundamentalists who wish to make the Southeast Asian nation an Islamic state.

Asia

Indonesia is the largest Muslim country in the world, followed by Pakistan, India, and Bangladesh. There are, in fact, many more non-Arab Muslims than Arab Muslims in the world; Indonesia's Muslim population of more than 200 million outnumbers all Arab Muslim populations combined. Correspondingly, while most Islamic fundamentalist thinking has its roots in Arab regions, fundamentalist movements in Southeast Asia, both moderate and militant, have significantly influenced the larger Muslim world and the way non-Muslims view Islamic fundamentalism. Militant movements in particular have taken shape in recent decades, most of them with some connection to militant training centers in Pakistan.

PAKISTAN

Founded as a country for Muslims in 1947, Pakistan has from the beginning been home to different forms of Islamic fundamentalism. Fundamentalists have played a central role in struggles over the relationship between Islam and politics, in training Islamic extremists to fight in Afghanistan and Kashmir, and in sectarian fighting between Sunnis and Shiites.

In the wake of British colonialism, the modernist Mohammed Ali Jinnah and the Muslim League argued that the Muslims and Hindus of India were in fact two separate nations, which led to the birth of Pakistan in 1947. Jinnah saw Islam as simply the common point of identity for Muslims and envisioned a secular country, but Pakistanis have never completely agreed on the question of whether Pakistan should be a state in which Muslims can practice their religion freely or an Islamic state relying on religious institutions and enforcing the Sharia. This tension is clear in the country's constitution, finalized in 1956, which provides for a parliamentary democracy but also calls the state the Islamic Republic of Pakistan and requires that the head of state be a Muslim.

Although he championed the cause of an independent nation for Muslims on the Indian subcontinent, Mohammed Ali Jinnah envisioned Pakistan as a secular state.

The country's leaders have alternately moved toward and retreated from state-sponsored Islamic law and institutions. Pakistani leaders have routinely used Islamic symbols and language to bolster their authority and policies, which has in turn strengthened the fundamentalist opposition. Fundamentalist groups like the Islamic Society have developed political parties and won some power through parliamentary elections, but most have operated outside the government as a force of resistance. The fundamentalists' influence has in many ways exceeded their relatively small numbers, which many attribute to the fact that Islam is the only common factor of identity for virtually all Pakistanis.

In contrast to the political parties, the Deobandis, a minority Sunni Muslim group in Pakistan whose teachings are similar to those of the Wahhabis, have fueled a more radical Islamic approach. The Deobandis originally formed in India in the mid-1800s, when a group deeply opposed to British rule gathered in the town of Deoband and founded schools for strict Muslim education of boys (*madrasas*). Some Deobandis moved to Pakistan in 1947, where they adopted a more radical stance, arguing against Western imperialism and opposing all forms of Western technology.

These neo-Deobandis founded *madrasas* for Afghan refugees in the vicinity of Peshawar in the Northwest Frontier Province. Many of the *madrasas* were run with Saudi Arabian funding (as a major financial supporter, Osama bin Laden visited Peshawar on numerous occasions), which brought with them a Wahhabi influence. The *madrasas* taught a rigid, militant worldview in which all unbelievers are considered **infidels** and open to attack. By 2001 there were 4,000 Deobandi *madrasas* in Pakistan.

The United States funneled money into Pakistan to train Islamic militants to fight in Afghanistan in the 1980s, and Pakistani agents trained the more promising *madrasa* students (*taliban*) at secret army camps. In 1996 it was *taliban* from Pakistan who formed the Taliban government in Afghanistan. Pakistani prime minister Benazir Bhutto supported the Taliban to prevent Afghanistan from being taken over by a pro-Indian government.

Pakistan has also trained militants to fight in the Kashmiri independence struggle against India, in which 30,000 have died since the late 1980s. Demanding that Kashmir be united with Pakistan and calling for the imposition of the Sharia, Pakistani militants have attracted scores of young Kashmiris to the cause.

To complicate the situation in Pakistan even further, Sunni and Shia Muslims are clashing there in increasingly violent ways. Historical tension between the two sects existed in India, especially when the British pitted the two groups against each other, but the conflict subsided in the early years of Pakistan's history. After the 1979 Iranian revolution, however, Iran helped the Pakistani Shiites organize a political party, while Saudi Arabia helped create militant anti-Shiite groups to prevent the spread of Iranian revolutionary thought. Since then, the Shia-Sunni struggle has taken on a life of its own, and hundreds have been killed in assassinations and reprisals. Sectarian militant groups so far have favored violent attack rather than participation in the political process.

After the al-Qaeda attacks of September 11, 2001, the Bush administration focused U.S. foreign policy on eliminating the international terrorist threat, and Pakistan's support of and training for militant groups came under scrutiny. Some groups have conducted terrorist campaigns against Westerners within Pakistan, and in its war on terrorism, the United States declared the largest group fighting India in Kashmir a terrorist organization. Pakistan's president, Pervez Musharraf, moved to adapt to the changing international climate.

Facing criticism within his own country for supporting the U.S. war in Afghanistan in 2001, Musharraf appealed to Islam as a modern religion of tolerance. He vowed to free Pakistan of militant extremism and sectarian violence, issued new regulations for the *madrasas*, and banned terrorist groups. However, in late 2002 a coalition of anti-American fundamentalist parties won elections in the Northwest Frontier Province and began implementing Islamic law. Also, many militant Pakistani groups simply reemerged under different names. On a positive note, in early

Pervez Musharraf pledged his country's cooperation in the U.S.-led fight against Islamic terrorism, and that support was likely the reason two attempts were made on the Pakistani president's life in late 2003. Pakistan—as host to many Saudi-funded and Wahhabist-influenced *madrasas*—has played a significant role in the spread of Islamic extremism.

2004 Musharraf and India's prime minister, Atal Bihari Vajpayee, met to discuss Kashmir, leading to hopes for a peaceful settlement in the disputed territory.

AFGHANISTAN

Beginning in the 1800s, Afghanistan, a Muslim country that borders Pakistan, thwarted the colonial schemes of both Great Britain and Russia for more than 100 years. In 1979 the Soviet Union invaded the rugged country in support of a communist regime that had seized power there. Over the following decade, Afghanistan was a major battlefield in the Cold War between the Soviet Union and the United States. The United States poured millions of dollars into arms and training for the *mujahedin*, Muslim guerrilla fighters from Afghanistan as well as other parts of the Islamic world. By 1989, unable to suppress mujahedin resistance, Soviet forces withdrew from Afghanistan, leaving a communist regime in place in the capital, Kabul. The leader of that regime agreed to step down in 1992, and an interim government was set up. But stability was not restored.

Rival Afghans fought for power, and former mujahedin commanders established themselves as warlords, controlling their own regions of the countryside. Many of the warlords were involved in illegal activities, and their treatment of the Afghan people was often bad.

A small group of mujahedin, many of them former students from the Pakistani *madrasas*, began their own resistance campaign. They received aid from Pakistan and came to be known as the Taliban. Many Afghans initially hailed the Taliban as heroes who would rein in the warlords and bring law and order to their war-torn country.

In 1995, however, the Taliban captured Kabul and made it clear that they intended to rule Afghanistan based on their blend of Wahhabist and neo-Deobandi views. By 1996 one of the Taliban's chief supporters, Osama bin Laden, had set up a camp in the Afghan mountains as his home base of operations.

Under the Taliban, official decisions were made in private by leader Mullah Muhammed Omar and a small group of Taliban elders, and the Sharia was implemented by the Ministry for the Promotion of Virtue and

Taliban fighters atop a tank, 1995. During its years in power, the Taliban imposed an extremely harsh interpretation of Sharia on Afghanistan's people. In late 2001, after its refusal to expel terrorist leader Osama bin Laden, the Taliban regime was toppled by a U.S.-led invasion.

Suppression of Vice (PVSV). The PVSV banned television, movies, and non-religious music; rigorously enforced public execution for homosexuality, adultery, and murder; and amputated the limbs of those convicted of robbery. Beating or flogging was prescribed for Afghan men who refused to grow beards and women who refused to wear *burqas*. Women's rights were especially affected under the Taliban. Women were forbidden to work outside the home or receive education, and they could not leave home or seek medical care without a male escort. The Taliban also conducted massacres of the Hazaras, the country's Shiite minority, saying they were not true Muslims.

Muslim religious leaders around the world condemned the Taliban's policies as contrary to Islam. International human rights organizations, Muslim nations from Iran to Egypt, and the U.N. denounced the Taliban for their violations of human rights. By 1999 only three countries—Pakistan, Saudi Arabia, and the United Arab Emirates—had officially recognized the Taliban government.

The Taliban's policies further worsened living conditions in Afghanistan. In 1999 the U.N. Security Council imposed sanctions on the Taliban for refusing to turn over bin Laden, who had been connected with several terrorist attacks against the United States, and Pakistan froze all Taliban assets within its borders. In 2000 the Taliban declared drug use contrary to Islam and banned Afghan farmers from growing poppies (used for the production of opium and heroin), leaving countless farmers and field laborers unemployed. The U.N. imposed further sanctions in 2001 as the Taliban continued to refuse to hand over bin Laden. The leadership of the Taliban became divided between those devoted to severe application of the Sharia and those who wanted more moderate laws in order to ease sanctions and address widening poverty in the country.

In 2001 the Taliban said statues were idolatrous according to Islam and ordered the destruction of all statues in Afghanistan. People around the world watched in shock as Taliban forces destroyed numerous pre-Islamic treasures, including two of the world's largest Buddhas, carved into cliffs in the Bamiyan province.

Taliban forces controlled most of Afghanistan by 2001. The only remaining opposition was the Northern Military Alliance (NMA). After the terrorist attacks on September 11, 2001, the United States focused international attention on the Taliban, charging them with offering safe haven to bin Laden, the alleged mastermind of the attacks. The Taliban denied that bin Laden had the resources to stage a terrorist operation of that magnitude, but in October 2001, the United States and Britain began a military campaign against the Taliban. By November the NMA had captured Kabul, and the Taliban surrendered in December. Mullah Omar and bin Laden are believed to have escaped into the network of caves near the Pakistani border, and as of early 2004 neither had been found. An interim government was installed under the protection of the U.N. Security Council, led by Taliban opponent Hamid Karzai, but Taliban remnants and renegade warlords continued to threaten the fledgling government.

CENTRAL ASIA

Central Asia occupies an area roughly the size of the United States, but has a population of only 70 million. It became a center of Islamic culture in the 10th century, especially in the Silk Road cities of Bukhara and Samarkand. Sufism later became a major influence. Russian takeover in the 1800s weakened Islamic institutions; Muslims practiced their rituals quietly, mosques were sparse, and the clergy was under the tight control of Russian (and later Soviet) supervisors. Under Soviet president Mikhail Gorbachev's reforms, however, the region saw an Islamic revival.

National identity was a new idea for Central Asians, who had relied on tribal and ethnic affiliations before the Russians took over, and the Soviet-backed governments faced little resistance after the Soviet Union collapsed. However, increasing population, scarcity of land and water, and poverty soon took their toll, opening the way for Islamic militants, many of whom are young and unemployed. Militant fundamentalism thus became one of the most effective ide-

A *madrasa* in Bukhara, Uzbekistan. Repressive measures by Uzbekistan's authoritarian leader, Islam Karimov, have thus far proved unsuccessful in stamping out Islamic fundamentalism in the former Soviet republic in Central Asia.

ologies for anti-government opposition. Militant groups have made some inroads in Turkmenistan, Kazakhstan, and Kyrgyzstan, but they have been most successful in Tajikistan and Uzbekistan.

In Tajikistan, the Islamic Revival Party of Tajikistan (IRP) emerged after independence and called for a democracy in which the transition to an Islamic state and the rule of the Sharia would take place gradually. By 1992 conflicts between the Russian-backed government and the IRP, along with ethnic and regional divisions, erupted into a civil war that killed 50,000 and lasted until 1997, at which time Islamic parties were granted a percentage of the seats in the parliament. Aware of the Taliban's misrule and worn down by war and poverty, Tajiks are suspicious of the fundamentalists, but an even more radical party, the Hizb-ut-Tahrir (HUT), is attracting new followers. The Soviet-style government is cracking down, but it seems wary of further empowering the militants by suppressing them too harshly.

Since 1991 Central Asia's largest country, Uzbekistan, has been governed by a Soviet-style leader, Islam Karimov. After claiming the presidency following elections that international observers considered seriously flawed, Karimov used various tactics to extend his term in office to 2007.

Karimov has conducted crackdowns and issued bans on the fundamentalist militant groups that sprang up after independence. In 1998 the Islamic Movement of Uzbekistan (IMU) declared its goal of establishing an Islamic state in Uzbekistan and eventually all of Central Asia; its leader was based in Peshawar, Pakistan, and had ties to bin Laden. In 1999 the IMU staged numerous incursions into Uzbekistan from its camps in Tajikistan, to which Karimov responded with another crackdown. IMU fighters later assisted Afghans in their war with the United States and were designated a terrorist organization by the U.S. State Department. In the meantime, Karimov's ban against fundamentalist groups means that any Muslim shown to have any connection with the groups can receive a jail sentence, and no Muslim man in the country is allowed to wear

Abu Rusdan, a leader of the Muslim extremist group Jemaah Islamiyah, sits in a courthouse cell in Jakarta, Indonesia, while awaiting his trial on charges stemming from the October 2002 bombing of a Bali nightclub. That attack killed more than 200 people.

a beard, as this is supposedly a sign of fundamentalist leanings.

The political battle against fundamentalist groups has led the United States and its international partners to provide aid to the poor countries of Central Asia. That aid has taken the form of economic support and military assistance in the battle against terrorism.

SOUTHEAST ASIA

The secular governments of Southeast Asia have prided themselves in recent decades on their pluralism, stability, and great strides toward modernization. But, like other Muslim countries that have experienced rapid growth, they have faced internal problems—poverty, government mismanagement, and religious tensions—that have resulted in fundamentalist opposition.

In recent years, this opposition has led to the growth of terrorist networks in Indonesia, Malaysia, Singapore, and the southern Philippines. Many of these terrorist groups have allegedly been aided by bin Laden. The groups have carried out deadly attacks in Bali, Indonesia, and in the Philippines. In Malaysia they allegedly helped plan the September 11, 2001, attacks on the United States.

A key network is Jemaah Islamiyah, based in Indonesia, which aspires to create an Islamic state that combines the Muslim countries Indonesia, Malaysia, Singapore, and Brunei, together with the Muslim portions of Thailand and the Philippines. Jemaah Islamiyah originally formed in the 1940s to seek the formation of an Islamic state in Indonesia. The group was reinvigorated in the 1990s, when Southeast Asian Muslims returned from fighting with the Afghans against Soviet occupation and brought bin Laden's influence with them.

Other networks include the Kumpulan Mujahideen in Malaysia and the Abu Sayyaf and the Moro Islamic Liberation Front in the southern Philippines. All condemn the U.S.-led war on terrorism and the U.S. invasions of Afghanistan and Iraq; they argue that the United States is in fact the biggest global threat because of its support of Israel and of un-Islamic regimes around the world.

Sub-Saharan Africa

Much of northern and east-central Africa, from Morocco in the west to Sudan and Somalia in the east, was absorbed in the early Islamic expansions of the seventh and eighth centuries and has long been considered part of the Arab world. But Muslim communities were established in other parts of Africa as far back as the seventh century. Today, nearly 20 percent of the world's Muslims, more than 200 million people, live in sub-Saharan Africa, and Islam is the fastest-growing religion on the continent. Nigeria alone has about 65 million Muslims.

Some historians suggest that the most rapid growth of Islam in Africa occurred at the height of European colonialism in the 20th century precisely because Islam provided a different worldview. This same search for an anti-Western alternative has fueled the rise of fundamentalism in the post-colonial and post–Cold War era. As world powers have stopped interfering in the governments of sub-Saharan African nations, corrupt politicians there have suppressed dissent, and poverty and old ethnic divisions have in many cases led to civil war. Social catastrophes, including famine and a growing AIDS crisis, afflict many countries. In countries with large Muslim populations, Islamic fundamentalists have often stepped into the breach, offering demoralized citizens hope for stability amidst the chaos. Nigeria provides the prime example.

NIGERIA

In Nigeria, as in the North African countries of Somalia and Sudan, Islamic leaders have implemented the Sharia for a variety of political and spiritual reasons, further complicating the country's already troubled religious, ethnic, and political landscape.

With a population of about 130 million, Nigeria is home to one-sixth of all Africans. Islam arrived in the country with Arab traders in the 13th century, and today approximately 50 percent of Nigerians, mostly of the Hausa and Fulani tribes, are Muslims. Europeans brought Christianity to southern Nigeria in the 15th century, and 40 percent of Nigerians now are Christians; most of them are either Protestants of the Yoruba tribe (in southwest Nigeria) or Roman Catholics of the Ibo tribe (in southeast Nigeria). The remainder of the population holds indigenous beliefs like *animism*.

When Nigeria won its independence from Britain in 1960, its new constitution acknowledged the divisions in the country by creating autonomous regions in the east, west, and north. However, this did not end ethnic and religious tensions, and beginning in 1966, civil war resulted in a series of military governments. In addition, huge increases in oil production in the country widened the divide between the wealthy and the poor. Finally, in

In response to the 1999 election of Olusegun Obasanjo, a Christian, to the presidency of Nigeria, a dozen predominantly Muslim states in the country's northern region announced the imposition of Sharia law.

1999, Olusegun Obasanjo, a Yoruba Christian from the south, became president in a democratic election and promised to end government corruption and poverty.

In answer to Obasanjo's election, the governor of the Nigerian state of Zamfara announced the implementation of Sharia rule, claiming that the switch to Islamic law was needed to stop corruption and poverty. The Sharia has since been implemented in 11 other states, so that approximately one-third of Nigerians now live under its rule. This has increased tensions between the largely Muslim north and the majority Christian south. In fact, since northerners largely dominated Nigerian politics from 1960 until Obasanjo's election, some critics accuse the northern leaders who have implemented the Sharia of deliberately trying to create factions in order to erode Obasanjo's influence and increase their own power, both within Nigeria and among oil-rich Arab states. Critics also say that poor people, particularly women, are being scapegoated to illustrate the success of the Sharia, while wealthier citizens and corrupt officials violate the law and go free.

Complicating the situation is the fact that poverty, illiteracy, and poor health care plague most of Nigeria and particularly the predominantly Muslim northern regions. Many Muslims therefore support implementation of the Sharia as a way to improve their living conditions. Their hope is that following Islamic law will increase political and economic stability, but since 1999, more than 6,000 Nigerians have died in religious fighting over Sharia

Amina Lawal (right), convicted by a Nigerian Sharia court of having a child out of wedlock, was sentenced in March 2002 to death by stoning. Amid a swirl of international protests, however, her sentence was overturned the following year.

rule. This has deepened the political conflict in the country, and some Muslim leaders have even gone so far as to call for the Sharia states to institute their own army to defend Muslims and the rule of Islamic law.

For centuries, the rulers of walled Muslim cities across northern Nigeria applied the Sharia in both civil and criminal cases. After the British colonized Nigeria in the late 1800s, however, the Sharia was applied only to personal matters. Now the religious police, known as the *Hizbah*, enforce Islamic law strictly in all areas of life. The penalty for murder is usually death, while the sentence for robbery is often amputation of a limb. Public drinking is punished with flogging, and gambling is also forbidden. Women live under strict conditions in their everyday lives; they must wear the *hijab*, cannot hold a job if they are unmarried, are not allowed to ride on motorcycles (a common mode of travel in Nigeria), have segregated bus stops, and cannot ride on buses with men. The *Hizbah* have also closed churches and non-Muslim schools, and in 2002 Zamfara began requiring all residents, including non-Muslims, to speak Arabic, a language few citizens know.

Sexual crimes also merit stiff penalties, especially for women. Conviction for sex outside marriage often results in a lashing, while sentencing for adultery can include death. The cases of two women in particular have gained international attention. In the state of Sokoto, Safiya Hussaini was found guilty of adultery and sentenced to death by stoning, but after she received global support, the ruling was overturned in early 2002. Also in 2002, in the state of Katsina, Amina Lawal was sentenced to death because she had a child while divorced. (The alleged father of her baby denied having sex with her and the charges against him were dropped.) In 2003 some contestants threatened to boycott the Miss World pageant in Nigeria because of the charges against Lawal, and the pageant was eventually staged in London. In September 2003 an appeals court overturned Lawal's death sentence.

As the Nigerian government seeks to maintain a democratic

process, the implementation of the Sharia and the resulting religious and ethnic conflicts will continue to complicate the national scene. During his first term, Obasanjo was unable to stabilize the country and ease the concerns of Muslims and Christians alike. Government corruption, poverty, and poor health care are still significant problems. Obasanjo was reelected in April 2003, but opposition groups from around the country complained about voting irregularities in the election process.

THE THREAT OF TERRORISM

The bombings of American embassies in Tanzania and Kenya in 1998 left 224 people dead. In Kenya in 2002, a suicide bombing killed 15 at a resort hotel, and other attackers narrowly missed hitting an Israeli plane with a shoulder-fired missile. In the wake of these attacks, observers around the world are watching to see if terrorist activity grows in sub-Saharan Africa.

Numerous sub-Saharan governments are plagued by political turmoil, among them Chad, the Republic of Congo, Liberia, and Sierra Leone. Many assert that conditions in these countries—erosion of cultural identity, economic deprivation, political repression, and corrupt, mismanaged governments—provide fertile ground for radical fundamentalism to take root and lead to increased terrorist activity. Some analysts link the recent attacks in the region to al-Qaeda and say Osama bin Laden and other militant leaders are taking advantage of the political turmoil in much the same way bin Laden was able to develop his organization in the uncontrolled environment of Afghanistan.

Even in somewhat more stable states like Kenya, Tanzania, and Mali, government forces are not able to police every area of the country. Observers say that lax security may make sub-Saharan Africa attractive for terrorist groups who want to operate unnoticed and attack vulnerable targets. National borders and inner-city areas are the least secure.

The underdeveloped economies in many African countries may

also make it easy to fund terrorism through activities such as money laundering and arms and diamond smuggling. Since terrorist groups operate in secret, however, only fragmentary information is available about their activities in these areas.

Only the future will tell if the chaos in African countries once dominated by Western powers will produce violent jihad groups like those in the Arab world and Central and Southeast Asia.

Scene from a ceremony held in New York City on the second anniversary of the September 11, 2001, terrorist attacks. By 2003 the United States had launched two wars, in Afghanistan and Iraq, in the name of stamping out the threat of Islamic terrorism.

The Western Response

In the wake of the September 11, 2001, attacks on the United States, analysts and ordinary citizens in the West have explored various explanations for why Islamic terrorist organizations are targeting the West. Many of these arguments, however, contradict one another, and no single argument sufficiently explains the complexities of Islamic fundamentalism or the Western response to it.

Some argue for swift and decisive military retaliation without dialogue, while others say the only lasting solution is increased exchange between Westerners and Islamic leaders around the world. Many make broad assumptions about the nature of Islam itself. Some, for example, maintain that Islam and the West are now engaged in a titanic battle between civilizations. Others say Islam is simply incompatible with the modern way of life, while still others argue that Islam is inherently violent and unjust. Some say Islam and democracy can never coexist, while others insist that Islamic democracies will work under the right conditions.

The central problem with the idea that the West and Islam are locked in an inevitable, global conflict is that Islam, like the West, is not easily defined as a single entity. Islam is in fact made up of Muslims who think differently about the relationship between their faith and politics, just as Westerners have different, shifting ideas about freedom, democracy, and the relationship between church and state. Similarly, the argument that Islam is by nature unjust belies the reality of different legal codes and freedoms in Muslim nations; women, for instance, are thought by some to be oppressed in all Muslim countries, when in fact the status of women varies from one country to the next, and women's status is often as affected by socioeconomic and cultural trends as by Islam. And the arguments that democracy and Islam do or do not mix often overlook the complexities of political rule in Muslim countries, where the chaos of post-colonialism has led to authoritarianism and where democratic projects have not been attempted at all or have been attempted only in ways that deny true participation from opposition groups, including fundamentalists.

However, most observers do agree that the United States and its allies must seriously weigh their responses to Islamic fundamentalism in general and to Islamic terrorist groups in particular. A critical first step in this process is to explore why Muslims, including fundamentalists, around the world think of the West, and particularly the United States, as they do.

MUSLIM ATTITUDES TOWARD THE WEST

Doubts among Muslims about Western intentions have their roots in the Crusades of the 11th through 13th centuries and in

European expansion beginning in the 19th century and continuing through World War I, when Europeans divided Islamic lands throughout the Middle East and Africa among themselves. This imperialism sowed the seeds for deep mistrust.

Now the preeminent world power is the United States. Though Muslims around the world admire American principles, many accuse the United States of hypocrisy. These Muslims say that,

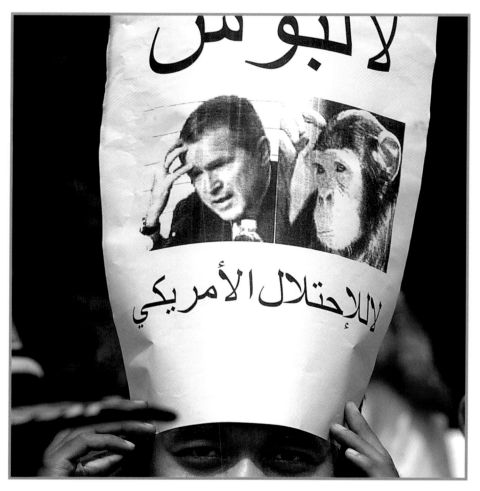

The juxtaposed pictures leave no doubt about this Indonesian Muslim's opinion of U.S. president George W. Bush. Many Muslims around the world viewed with suspicion and contempt the Bush administration's policies in its "war on terror."

while the United States is not overtly colonizing Muslim lands, in its dealings with the Muslim world it fails to apply the principles it holds dear for its own citizens.

In the Muslim view, the high point of U.S. hypocrisy is its uncritical support for Israel. This issue, more than any other, unites Muslims around the world in their mistrust of the United States. Surveys in the Arab world show that a majority of Muslims feel that the Palestinian issue is an important, or even the most important, issue they face as Muslims; surveys of Muslims in the United States show strong support for a Palestinian state. As the United States backs what Muslims view as Israel's repressive policies in the occupied territories and looks the other way while Israel violates U.N. resolutions, Muslims cry foul and accuse the United States of ignoring its own principles when convenient.

Similar charges of hypocrisy have been leveled at the United States for punishing Iraq and Pakistan, both Muslim countries, for having nuclear weapons programs without insisting that India and Israel also gut their programs. Muslims also condemn what they view as the slow response of the United States to Serbian campaigns of "ethnic cleansing" against Bosnian Muslims and Kosovar Muslims during the 1990s, as well as the U.S. refusal to take strong action to halt the repression of Muslims in Kashmir and Chechnya.

While many Islamic fundamentalists decry Western influence in general, and while Wahhabis like Osama bin Laden vow holy war against Western infidels, the vast majority of Muslims around the world do not see Westerners as evil. However, some suggest that the rhetoric of good versus evil as a way to increase support for the West's "war on terror" may have the effect, intentional or not, of increasing mistrust among Muslims worldwide. President George W. Bush's identification of Iran and Iraq (along with North Korea) as an "axis of evil" in his State of the Union address in January 2002 provides one potent example.

THE HISTORY OF THE U.S. RESPONSE

U.S. policy toward Islamic fundamentalism first took shape during World War II, when President Franklin D. Roosevelt sent U.S. troops to protect Saudi Arabia. This close relationship continued through the Cold War and the 1970s and 1980s, even as the two countries disagreed over Israel. In 1990 the United States based a military force in Saudi Arabia that numbered in the thousands and remained until 2003, when all but a few hundred troops were pulled out. The ties with the Saudi government have given the United States access to the vast oil reserves in the Persian Gulf region and a base for opposing first Iran and later Iraq. The United States has continued this relationship in spite of international condemnation of the Saudi monarchy's violations of human rights. The Saudi government has also been a primary sponsor, using its enormous oil funds, of fundamentalist Islamic movements worldwide, including militant groups like Hamas and the Taliban.

In spite of its intimate relationship with Saudi Arabia, after the Iranian revolution of 1979 the United States gradually began to shift from its Cold War opposition to Arab nationalists to a fight against Islamic fundamentalism as a political force. After Khomeini came to power, fundamentalist groups throughout the Islamic world stepped up their criticism of Western influence, while militant groups actively resisted pro-West governments and the United States itself. The West was shocked when militants in Tehran held 49 American embassy workers hostage for 444 days, and the Iranian-backed attacks against U.S. and French troops in Beirut in 1983, which killed more than 300 soldiers, brought the suicide bombing into American consciousness.

Many U.S. policy makers began to concentrate on Islamic extremism as representative of Islam in general, and the United States supported a number of the nationalist governments it had once opposed as they suppressed more moderate fundamentalist groups that sought to participate in the political process. From

For many Americans, the 1979–1981 hostage crisis in Tehran provided a first ominous glimpse of Islamic fundamentalism.

Egypt to Indonesia, from Algeria to the Philippines, national leaders repressed fundamentalist resistance, and in the process won U.S. military and economic aid. In many instances, however, the repressive response of these governments only strengthened and further radicalized fundamentalist groups.

Meanwhile, the Cold War between the United States and the Soviet Union also fueled the growth of militant Islamic fundamentalism. While the administration of President Ronald Reagan had attempted to isolate Iran for its fundamentalist leadership, it actively funded the training of the 20,000-strong mujahedin in Afghanistan to contain Soviet expansion in the region. The nucleus of current international Islamic terrorist networks was in many ways formed in that conflict, when fighters were trained in Pakistan and thousands of Arabs fought in Afghanistan under the influence of Osama bin Laden, who himself had strong connections with the U.S. Central Intelligence Agency at that time. After the Soviet withdrawal, the United States disengaged from Afghanistan as well, and many Arab fighters felt betrayed. They subsequently returned to their own countries to establish or contribute to militant movements there. The United States then put pressure on the governments of Muslim countries to rein in these militant movements, to which some leaders responded with frustration given that the United States had itself earlier financed the militants.

In 1991 the United States and a coalition that included European and Persian Gulf states expelled Iraq from Kuwait, which Iraq had invaded the previous year. While oil-rich Persian Gulf governments did aid the war effort, many Muslims within these countries and throughout the world protested the U.S.-led attack on a Muslim country. Combined with rising tensions in Israel and the occupied territories, where Palestinians had begun the first *intifada*, the Gulf War and the presence of American and European soldiers on Saudi Arabian soil reinforced Islamic fundamentalists' belief in the anti-Muslim, interventionist intentions of the West.

President Bill Clinton continued President George Bush's pursuit of secure access to oil, though he did promote the 1993 Oslo Accords between Israel and the PLO, and he more carefully distinguished between moderate and militant fundamentalists. Concerns about Islamic extremism rose rapidly, however, as terrorist attacks increased through the 1990s. Among the targets bombed were the World Trade Center in 1993, U.S. military installations in Saudi Arabia in 1996, the American embassies in Kenya and Tanzania in 1998, and the USS *Cole* in Yemen in 2000. Osama bin Laden was suspected to be behind these attacks, and after his name appeared on the FBI's Most Wanted list in 1998, the United States bombed his training camps in Afghanistan and Somalia. More and more, Western lawmakers and policy analysts interpreted the Muslim world through the lens of extremist activity.

THE RESPONSE SINCE SEPTEMBER 11, 2001

In the wake of the terrorist attacks on September 11, 2001, Western policies on Islamic fundamentalism have increasingly been characterized by two strains of thought. The first blames Islamic fundamentalists, rather than secular regimes, for the widespread lack of development and democracy in the Muslim world and for the terrorist networks now threatening Western targets. This strain of thought favors crackdowns on fundamentalist movements. The second strain of thought advocates diplomacy to encourage more open political processes in Muslim countries and thereby decrease terrorist activity.

The administration of President George W. Bush has largely been characterized by the more confrontational approach, which has been popular with many Americans (though not with as many Europeans). After September 11, 2001, President Bush immediately declared an international "war on terror" to wipe out the threat of terrorism worldwide, and the U.N. Security Council passed a resolution condemning the attacks on U.S. soil and calling on all nations to bring those behind the attacks to justice. In an effort to root out Osama bin Laden, a U.S.-led coalition invaded Afghanistan just two months after the September attacks. When the United States and Britain invaded Iraq in March 2003, the justification for the war rested largely on the assertion that Saddam Hussein had weapons of mass destruction that he might shift to terrorist groups. Numerous European countries, including France and Germany, condemned the invasion of Iraq, while Muslim fundamentalists around the world interpreted the latest use of Western military force as a fresh assault on Islam, a view that some observers predict could have the effect of increasing rather than weakening the appeal of fundamentalist movements.

Meanwhile, international human rights groups are concerned that the war on terror is giving leaders in numerous countries an excuse to severely repress Islamic fundamentalist groups. An area of special concern is Central Asia, where the leaders of Tajikistan, Uzbekistan, and Kazakhstan are taking a harder line against opposition groups as the United States funds a stronger military presence in the region. Concerns are also being raised about recent clampdowns on alleged terrorist activities in Chechnya, Egypt,

Malaysia, and Saudi Arabia and anti-terror laws passed in Indonesia, India, Singapore, and Tanzania.

In addition to military access and government stability, oil continues to be a key factor in U.S. and European policy. The United States and its allies first developed close relationships with Persian Gulf countries to ensure a steady supply of oil to the West, and a central objective of the Gulf War was to secure Kuwaiti oil fields. Perhaps not surprisingly, critics have charged the Bush administration with being more concerned about access to oil than fearful of weapons of mass destruction. Oil will continue to affect U.S. and European relations with countries where Islamic fundamentalist movements exist. The United States, for example, is increasingly looking to Nigeria and other countries in West Africa as a source for oil imports to offset reliance on the Middle East, a relationship the Bush administration fears will be threatened by increasing Islamic fundamentalism in the region.

THE FUTURE

As the threat of terrorism continues, the challenge for the United States and other Western countries will be to deal with the complexities within fundamentalist Islam and within Islam itself. Future policy makers will continue to choose between the use of military and financial strength to stop fundamentalist movements and the exercise of diplomacy to encourage more open political processes and economic development in Muslim countries.

In the meantime, Muslims around the world are waiting to see if democracy emerges in Iraq as promised and if a final peace deal can be successfully brokered between Israel and a new Palestinian state. The outcome of these and other situations in which Western and Islamic interests intersect will shape Islamic fundamentalism and the Western response to it for decades to come.

Chronology

1303 Taqi al-Din Ahmad ibn Taymiyya instructs Muslims to revolt against their Mongol rulers for not being faithful to Islam.

1745 Muhammad ibn Abd al-Wahhab and Muhammad ibn Saud forge an alliance and declare war on any who do not follow the straight path of Islam.

1904 The British discover oil in Iran.

1924 In the wake of the collapse of the Ottoman Empire, the caliphate is abolished.

1928 Hasan al-Banna establishes the Muslim Brotherhood in Egypt.

1932 Saudi Arabia is established as the first modern Islamic state.

1938 Oil is discovered in Saudi Arabia.

1941 Mawlana Mawdudi establishes the Islamic Society of India.

1947 Pakistan is founded as a country for Muslims.

1948 Israel becomes a nation.

1965 Sayyid Qutb publishes his book *Milestones* in Egypt; he is executed one year later.

1967 Israel defeats Egypt, Jordan, and Syria in the Six-Day War.

1973 Egypt wins some battles in the 1973 October War with Israel, and OPEC stages an oil embargo.

1979 Ayatollah Ruhollah Khomeini declares Iran an Islamic state, and Osama bin Laden joins other Arabs fighting the Soviet occupation of Afghanistan.

1987 The first Palestinian *intifada* against the Israeli presence in the West Bank and Gaza Strip begins; the militant Islamic group Hamas is founded.

Chronology

1991 The United States defeats Iraq in the Gulf War and keeps U.S. troops in Saudi Arabia.

1996 The Taliban takes control of Afghanistan.

2000 The second Palestinian *intifada* begins, damaging the Israeli-Palestinian peace process.

2001 Terrorist attacks on U.S. soil kill more than 3,000, and the United States invades Afghanistan and overthrows the Taliban.

2003 The United States invades Iraq and topples the secular government of Saddam Hussein.

Glossary

animism—the belief that all natural phenomena have souls and can influence human events.

apostasy—the renunciation of one's religious or political beliefs.

autocratic—characteristic of a ruler with unlimited power.

ayatollah—a religious leader of Shiite Muslims.

bazaar—an area of small shops and people selling various goods.

burqa—a robe for women that covers the body from head to toe, with only a grid over the eyes through which to see.

caliphate—the dominion of the chief Muslim ruler, who is regarded as a successor of Muhammad.

coup—a sudden, illegal, often violent seizure of government.

Druze—a Middle Eastern religion characterized by monotheism and a belief in al-Hakim (985–1021) as the embodiment of God.

fatwa—a legal opinion or decree issued by an Islamic religious leader.

Hadith—the body of customs, sayings, and traditions ascribed to the prophet Muhammad.

ideological—relating to the beliefs on which an organization or political system is based.

Imam—in the Shiite tradition, one of the historical leaders descended from Muhammad and considered to be the divinely appointed and infallible successors of the Prophet; broadly, a Muslim spiritual leader.

indigenous—originating in a place rather than arriving from another place.

Glossary

infidels—any who do not accept the religious faith of the person speaking.

intifada—an uprising against Israeli rule among Palestinians of the Gaza Strip and West Bank.

Mahdi—according to Shiite belief, the 12th and last Imam, who has been hidden from humanity's view for centuries but will reappear to usher in a period of justice before Judgment Day.

Marxism—a set of social, political, and economic principles advocated by Karl Marx, including common ownership of means of production.

Sharia—Islamic law.

sultan—a ruler of a Muslim country.

umma—the worldwide community of Muslims.

Further Reading

Armstrong, Karen. *The Battle for God.* New York: Ballantine, 2001.

Esposito, John L. *Unholy War: Terror in the Name of Islam.* New York: Oxford University Press, 2002.

Hiro, Dilip. *War Without End: The Rise of Islamist Terrorism and the Global Response.* New York: Routledge, 2002.

Murphy, Caryle. *Passion for Islam: Shaping the Modern Middle East: The Egyptian Experience.* New York: Scribner, 2002.

Rashid, Ahmed. *Taliban: Militant Islam, Oil and Fundamentalism in Central Asia.* New Haven, Conn.: Yale University Press, 2001.

Schwartz, Stephen. *The Two Faces of Islam: The House of Sa'ud from Tradition to Terror.* New York: Doubleday, 2002.

Wright, Robin. *The Last Great Revolution: Turmoil and Transformation in Iran.* New York: Knopf, 2000.

Internet Resources

http://nmhschool.org/tthornton/summahry.htm

Comprehensive exploration of key figures and events in Islamic fundamentalism.

http://www.masmn.org/Books/

Electronic versions of books by fundamentalist thinkers, including al-Banna, Mawdudi, and Qutb.

http://www.fordham.edu/halsall/islam/islamsbook.html

Islamic history site that includes profiles of Muslim countries and links to important documents since 1945.

http://www.arches.uga.edu/~godlas/islamwest.html

Extensive links to essays on Islamic fundamentalism and terrorism.

http://www.islamfortoday.com/fundamnetalism.htm

Collection of articles by Muslims arguing against Islamic fundamentalism.

http://www.arabworldnews.com

Comprehensive news of the Arab world, with links to news sources throughout the region.

http://www.metimes.com/

Weekly news and analysis of politics, business, religion, and culture in the Middle East.

http://www.fmep.org/

Website of the Foundation for Middle East Peace, a nonprofit organization that provides up-to-date information on the Israeli-Palestinian conflict.

Index

Numbers in **bold italic** refer to captions.

Index

Index

Index

Picture Credits

3: Choo Youn-Kong/AFP/Getty Images
8: Abdullah Y. Al-Dobais/Saudi Aramco World/PADIA
11: Nik Wheeler/Saudi Aramco World/PADIA
12: Kevin Bubriski/Saudi Aramco World/PADIA
16: Dick Doughty/Saudi Aramco World/PADIA
18: Burnett H. Moody/Saudi Aramco World/PADIA
25: Bettmann/Corbis
28: Hulton/Archive/Getty Images
30: AFP/Corbis
33: Hulton/Archive/Getty Images
34: Hulton/Archive/Getty Images
38: Hulton/Archive/Getty Images
41: Bettmann/Corbis
42: Hulton/Archive/Getty Images
43: Philippe Desmazes/AFP/Getty Images
44: S. M. Amin/Saudi Aramco World/PADIA
46: Marco Di Lauro/Getty Images
49: Hulton/Archive/Getty Images
52: S.M. Amin/Saudi Aramco World/PADIA

54: U.S. Department of Defense
57: Federal Bureau of Investigation
58: Dick Doughty/Saudi Aramco World/PADIA
63: Hulton/Archive/Getty Images
64: Jimmy Carter Presidential Library
66: Courtney Kealy/Getty Images
70: Vincenzo Pinto/AFP/Getty Images
73: Hulton/Archive/Getty Images
76: Abid Katib/Getty Images
78: Adek Berry/AFP/Getty Images
80: Hulton/Archive/Getty Images
83: Kim Jae-Hwan/AFP/Getty Images
84: Robert Nickelsburg/Time Life Pictures/Getty Images
87: Tor Eigeland/Saudi Aramco World/PADIA
88: Indra/Getty Images
90: Simon Maina/AFP/Getty
93: Pius Utomi Ekpei/AFP/Getty Images
94: Pius Utomi Ekpei/AFP/Getty Images
98: Mike Segar-Pool/Getty Images
101: Bay Ismoyo/AFP/Getty
104: Hulton/Archive/Getty Images

Cover: AFP/Corbis; **back cover:** Dick Doughty/Saudi Aramco World/PADIA

Contributors

General Editor **DR. KHALED ABOU EL FADL** is one of the leading authorities in Islamic law in the United States and Europe. He is currently a visiting professor at Yale Law School as well as Professor of Law at the University of California, Los Angeles (UCLA). He serves on the Board of Directors of Human Rights Watch, and regularly works with various human rights organizations, such as the Lawyer's Committee for Human Rights and Amnesty International. He often serves as an expert witness in international litigation involving Middle Eastern law, and in cases involving terrorism, national security, immigration law and political asylum claims.

Dr. Abou El Fadl's books include *The Place of Tolerance in Islam* (2002); *Conference of the Books: The Search for Beauty in Islam* (2001); *Rebellion in Islamic Law* (2001); *Speaking in God's Name: Islamic Law, Authority, and Women* (2001); and *And God Knows the Soldiers: The Authoritative and Authoritarian in Islamic Discourse* (second edition, revised and expanded, 2001).

Dr. Abou El Fadl was trained in Islamic legal sciences in Egypt, Kuwait, and the United States. After receiving his bachelors degree from Yale University and law degree from the University of Pennsylvania, he clerked for Arizona Supreme Court Justice J. Moeller. While in graduate school at Princeton University, where he earned a Ph.D. in Islamic Law he practiced immigration and investment law in the United States and the Middle East. Before joining the UCLA faculty in 1998, he taught at the University of Texas at Austin, Yale Law School, and Princeton University.

General Editor **DR. JOHN CALVERT** is assistant professor of history at Creighton University. He is interested in social protest and political resistance movements in the Arab world during the 19th and 20th centuries, and his current research focuses on the intellectual career and cultural milieu of Sayyid Qutb (1906–1966), the prominent Egyptian ideologue of Islamism.

A member of the faculty at Creighton since 1994, Dr. Calvert teaches a variety of courses relating to the medieval and modern periods of Middle East history. He earned a Ph.D. in Islamic Studies from McGill University in Montreal. His published articles include "Mythic Foundations of Radical Islam" (*Orbis*, Winter 2004); "Sayyid Qutb and the Power of Political Myth: Insights from Sorel" (*Historical Reflections/Reflexions Historiques*, 2004); "The Islamist Syndrome of Cultural Confrontation" (*Orbis*, Spring 2002); and "The Nation and the Individual: Sayyid Qutb's Tifl min al-Qarya (Child from the Village)" (*The Muslim World*, Spring 2000).

KIM WHITEHEAD is a writer, editor, and teacher. She has worked with numerous religious non-profits and holds an M.Div. and a Ph.D. in religion and literature. She lives in Mississippi with her husband and son.